DISCOVER BRUNCH:

A New Way of Entertaining

By Ruth Macpherson

HAMMOND®
INCORPORATED
MAPLEWOOD, NEW JERSEY 07040

Library of Congress Cataloging in Publication Data

Macpherson, Ruth.
　Discover brunch.

　1. Brunches.　I. Title.
TX733.M36　　641.5'3　　76-30683
ISBN 0-8437-2110-3

Printed in the United States of America.

Cover Photo:
Apple Sausage Ring, Page 26.

Introduction

For as long as I can remember, I have loved entertaining. My first experience was planning a party for my 6th-grade teacher. I felt a little self-conscious, but I remember a real feeling of satisfaction when the party was over. This self-fulfillment has stayed with me through many years and many, many parties.

While I was living as a single girl in New York City, San Francisco and Hawaii, some of my happiest experiences were organizing showers, birthday and going away parties, brunches, lunches and dinners; always experimenting with different ways to prepare and present · foods. To me, both facets of food presentations — making the food and setting it out — go together and each is as important as the other. Then I married a man who regards entertaining as one of his favorite hobbies!

Schools, religious and civic organizations always need people to run their fund raisers. I found myself volunteering for those activities involving the planning and service of food — and loving the work. As an outgrowth of these experiences, I began a catering business which has proved to be a great success and lots of fun.

When I examined each phase of my cooking career, brunches kept appearing in the foreground. I have discovered that no other type of entertaining offers host and hostess the flexibility of the brunch! The number of people to be served, the type of menu, the time of day and the theme of the party all fit well into a brunch. From an intimate sit-down meal to a large buffet party, the brunch can handle it, and so can you. The variety of menus is endless — from the elegant ease of a puffy soufflé or the simplicity of toasty English muffins and fried eggs to a hearty spinach and egg casserole. Anything goes.

And best of all, a brunch can make it possible for the host and especially the hostess to enjoy their party with their guests. Most of my menus can either be prepared ahead or feature foods that can be cooked at the last minute.

Brunches are flexible! If the meeting runs a little late, or the home team wins quickly, it doesn't make a bit of difference. Guests can easily be served within an hour of their arrival — and, incidentally, they should be!

No matter what the occasion, it can be celebrated with brunch. Out-of-town wedding guests will love an introduction before the big event or appreciate a send-off the following morning. And is there any better way to get old friends together than to watch their alma mater play in the Rose Bowl?

Plain or fancy, early or late, big or small, brunches are best! Discover this for yourself by letting me help you with parties which will be great successes.

First, I would like to thank my parents for teaching me to appreciate beautifully prepared and served meals and for training me in their preparation. They are both gourmet cooks and made me aware from childhood of the importance of well balanced, good tasting and attractively presented foods. And to Malcolm, Macky and Jeannie a million thanks for your interest and food-tasting expertise. I want to add a special thanks to my long-time friend, Barbara Hull, for her help in getting the book written.

Contents

Contents

JANUARY

NEW YEAR'S DAY BRUNCH
Serves 12

Whiskey Sours *
Cheese Straws *
Oyster Bisque *
Ham and Spinach Rolls *
Company Eggs
Baked Peaches *
Dream Bars **
Coffee and Tea

New Year's Day is a favorite time to get some of your husband's college friends together for brunch while watching their alma mater play in the Rose Bowl. One thing is certain, you will not have to worry about their entertaining themselves while you are in and out of the kitchen! Plan your party for your den or basement so your guests can eat and watch television comfortably. Have your husband mix up a large batch of Whiskey Sours and keep the pitcher handy. The soup course, mugs of steaming Oyster Bisque, can be served to them from a tray during the first quarter of the game. Cheese Straws can be passed at the same time. Put them within easy reach. The rest of the food requires little last minute attention, so you will not have to worry about leaving the game at a crucial point.

Table Setting

Your table decorations can be made easy because of your school football and New Year's Day theme. Hang balloons, party horns and streamers in the school colors. Underneath use a tablecloth which will go well with your colors. Make a nest of greens and colorful pompon chrysanthemums around a football in the middle of your table. Wrap your forks in napkins to match your tablecloth and tie them with wool in the school colors. With this bright and busy table setting, plain china will be best.

*Do ahead
**Freeze

Whiskey Sours

The following is a very easy way to make these drinks. Make as many as you want. For 12 ample drinks:

3 cans frozen lemonade
   concentrate
3 lemonade cans of
   bourbon, rye, or
   Scotch
1½ lemonade cans of
   water
lots of ice

lemon slices (garnish)
maraschino cherries (garnish)

Pour all ingredients except fruits for garnish in a large pitcher; stir well. Also good when done in a blender. Fill whiskey sour glasses or short old-fashioned glasses and garnish with a lemon slice and a cherry.

Cheese Straws

Make lots of these, since people love them and will probably eat more than you think. Makes about 7 dozen straws.

1 stick piecrust mix
½ cup (2 ounces)
   shredded sharp
   Cheddar cheese
salt
poppy or caraway
   seeds
paprika

Heat oven to 450°. Prepare pastry for 9-inch, one-crust pie as directed on package, except stir in cheese with hot water. Roll into a rectangle, 13 × 10 inches; place on ungreased baking sheet. With sharp knife, cut lengthwise into 3 strips, then crosswise. (Do not separate strips; they will bake apart.) Sprinkle with salt, seeds and paprika. Bake 8-10 minutes or until golden brown. Serve hot or cold. Straws can be prepared ahead of time and refrigerated on baking sheet; bake just before serving.

Oyster Bisque

This can be made ahead of time. Just reheat before serving. A real treat. Serves 12.

¾ cup uncooked rice
1½ quarts bottled clam
   juice
6 tablespoons butter
3 dozen oysters
½ scant teaspoon hot
   pepper sauce

3 cups light cream
6 tablespoons cognac
salt and pepper
chopped parsley for
   garnish

Cook rice in clam juice, covered, until very soft. Add butter. Whirl in blender. Finely chop 24 oysters or whirl in blender with their liquid. Add to rice mixture with hot pepper sauce. Stir in cream and heat just to boiling point. Add 12 oysters and heat until they just curl at the edges. Add cognac and heat 1 minute. Season with salt and pepper to taste. Ladle into heated mugs, putting a whole oyster in each mug. Garnish with chopped parsley.

Ham and Spinach Rolls

This lovely dish came from my Aunt Helen in Sarasota, Florida. Many of her fine recipes have been passed along to my mother and then to me. This is different, delicious, and easy to prepare.
Makes 24 rolls; allow 2 per person.

24 thin slices boiled ham (#4 on slicing machine)
2 packages (10 ounces each) frozen
chopped spinach, cooked and drained
2 cups packaged cornbread stuffing
2 cups sour cream

Cream Sauce:
8 tablespoons butter
8 tablespoons flour
4 cups milk
paprika
grated Parmesan cheese
½ cup grated sharp Cheddar cheese

Combine spinach, stuffing and cream. Spread on ham. Roll up and place seam-side-down in casserole. Melt butter in a saucepan; add flour and blend well. Add milk and continue stirring over medium-high heat until thick. Add cheese and remove from heat. Stir until all the cheese is melted. Pour over ham. Sprinkle with paprika and a little grated Parmesan cheese. Bake at 350° for 15 minutes covered and another 15 minutes uncovered.

Company Eggs

This is so easy, especially since the eggs are baked in the oven and served from the same dish. Serves 12.

½ pound Gruyère cheese, grated
4 tablespoons butter
1 cup heavy cream
½ teaspoon salt
dash pepper
1½ teaspoons dry mustard
12 eggs, slightly beaten

Spread cheese in buttered 13 × 9-inch baking dish. Dot with butter. Mix cream with seasonings and mustard. Pour half over cheese. Add slightly beaten eggs, and then add remaining half of cream mixture. Bake at 325° for about 35 minutes or until eggs are set.

11

Baked Peaches

These go well with ham and are easy to do. ½ peach for each serving.

12 canned or fresh
   peach halves
2 tablespoons butter
4 tablespoons sugar
lemon juice
cinnamon

Fill each peach cavity with ½ teaspoon butter, 1 teaspoon sugar, a sprinkling of lemon juice, and a dusting of cinnamon. Place in baking dish and bake at 350° for 20 minutes.

Dream Bars

Chewy, delicious and easy to make. Freeze well. Makes about 2½ dozen, 3 × 1-inch bars.

½ cup butter, softened
   or melted
½ cup light brown
   sugar (packed)
1 cup flour

Topping:

2 eggs, well beaten
1 cup light brown
   sugar (packed)
1 teaspoon vanilla
2 tablespoons flour
1 teaspoon baking
   powder
½ teaspoon salt
1 cup shredded
   coconut
1 cup thin-sliced al-
   monds

Heat oven to 350°. Mix butter and ½ cup sugar thoroughly. Stir in 1 cup flour. Press and flatten with hand to cover bottom of ungreased 13x9½x2-inch baking dish. Bake 10 minutes. Mix eggs, sugar and vanilla. Mix with flour, baking powder and salt. Stir in coconut and almonds. Spread this topping over baked crust. Return to oven and bake 25 minutes more, or until golden brown. Cool slightly, then cut in bars.

A BRUNCH FOR FRIENDS PASSING THROUGH TOWN
Serves 4–6

International Coffee
**Marinated Oranges *
**Creamed Eggs with Ham *
Onion English Muffins
**Tomatoes Stuffed with Mushrooms *

An unexpected call from friends who are traveling is a nice surprise. When they say they will be in your area early the next day, this is your opportunity to invite them for brunch. Since you want to spend time visiting with your out-of-town guests, your work in the kitchen will be before they come. They probably will not want an alcoholic drink since they will be driving for the rest of the day, so this is a great time to serve a special coffee drink. On short notice it's nice to be able to prepare one very special item. The marinated oranges take a little extra time but are well worth the effort. They're delicious. The menu serves 4–6 persons (in case they forgot to mention if their children were traveling with them). This brunch can be served either in the dining room or the kitchen, wherever you feel most comfortable.

Table Setting
Wherever you choose to eat, you can use a houseplant in a pretty container in the center of your table. Pretty placemats and matching napkins to enhance your good china and silver will make your guests feel welcome.

 * Do ahead
** Freeze

International Coffee
A little different, easy and good. Makes 6 servings.

⅓ cup instant cocoa
   mix
¼ cup instant coffee
4 cups boiling water
whipped cream,
   sweetened

Mix all the ingredients except the whipped cream in a heatproof container. Pour into coffee mugs and top with sweetened whipped cream.

Marinated Oranges

You and your guests will love this elegant dish. Serves 6.

8 large navel oranges
4 cups water
¼ cup Grand Marnier
  or curaçao
2 cups sugar
⅔ cup water

Remove just the orange part of skin of oranges with a vegetable parer. Cut pared strips into thin slivers 1½-2 inches long. Put in saucepan with 4 cups water. Simmer 20 minutes or until tender. Drain; rinse in cold water; drain well. Add liqueur; let stand. Remove all white membrane from oranges and cut into ½-inch slices. Combine sugar and ⅔ cup water in a saucepan. Cook over medium heat until candy thermometer registers 244°F. Remove from heat. Arrange oranges on serving dish. Spoon syrup over oranges, a spoonful at a time, to glaze them. Drain orange rind; reserve liqueur. Top glazed oranges with slivers of rind. Garnish with small pieces of fresh mint, if desired. Chill. Just before serving, pour reserved liqueur around oranges.

Creamed Eggs with Ham

You can do this ahead of time and keep in the top of a double boiler on very low heat. Serve on split English muffins. Serves 6.

6 hard-cooked eggs,
  sliced or chopped
1½ cups chopped ham

White Sauce:

4 tablespoons butter
4 tablespoons flour
2 cups milk
½ teaspoon salt
¼ teaspoon pepper

Melt butter and blend in flour. Add milk gradually, stirring constantly until it comes to a boil. Reduce heat and cook 3 minutes longer; add seasonings, chopped ham and eggs. Serve or keep warm in top of double boiler.

English Muffins with Onion

These are very tasty. Just split, toast and butter. Make plenty so that you can also enjoy them with crabapple jelly.

Tomatoes Stuffed with Mushrooms

These can be made ahead and then heated before serving. Serves 6.

6 medium tomatoes
1 pint fresh mush-
  rooms, chopped
3 tablespoons butter
½ cup sour cream
2 egg yolks, beaten
¼ cup fine, dry bread
  crumbs
1 teaspoon salt
dash pepper
dash thyme
3 tablespoons fine, dry
  bread crumbs

Cut stem end from tomatoes; scoop out pulp. Turn shells upside-down to drain. Chop pulp fine; measure 1 cup; set aside. Cook mushrooms in 2 tablespoons butter until tender. Combine sour cream and egg yolks. Add to mushrooms with the tomato pulp; mix well. Stir in the crumbs, salt, pepper and thyme. Cook and stir until mixture thickens and boils. Place tomato shells in 10 × 6-inch flat baking dish. Spoon mushroom mixture into tomatoes. Combine 1 tablespoon melted butter and 3 tablespoons fine, dry bread crumbs; sprinkle atop tomatoes. Bake at 375° for 25 minutes.

A PADDLE TENNIS INTERMISSION BRUNCH

Serves 18

Hot Buttered Rum*
Cheddar Fondue Cubes **
Creamed Chipped Beef in Patty Shells *
Orange Sherbet Salad Mold *
Crudités *
(Carrots, Celery, etc.)
Date Nut Bread **
Fudge Ring **
Coffee

With only an hour and a half between tournaments, your guests will want to be warmed up and fed brunch quickly. Hot Buttered Rum served in ceramic mugs is a perfect drink for a cold January day. Mugs are easy to hold while your guests are stretching their legs and chatting after an exciting match. The Chipped Beef, which is both attractive and delicious, can be cooked ahead and left warming when you go to the match. Keep a large kettle or pan filled with hot water so you can mix the toddies on your arrival. The Fudge Ring will look very tempting and can be eaten without a plate and fork.

Table Setting

For your centerpiece fill a large wooden salad bowl with greens and dowels of various lengths with vibrant orange and yellow paddle balls stuck on the ends. Stick the greens and dowels into styrene plastic which has been attached to your bowl with florist's clay. For your tablecloth do something unique! Buy a brightly patterned sheet (a double-flat will do it) in gay colors to complement the paddle balls. Paper napkins the color of the balls and white dishes will complete a very gay table. Stack your pastry shells on a large platter and place it next to a chafing dish for the Chipped Beef. This occasion calls for a bright and cheerful table, and you will receive many compliments on your ingenuity.

*Do ahead
**Freeze

Hot Buttered Rum

This can be made quite easily. Have all the ingredients in the mugs ahead of time and at the last minute pour in boiling water. For an individual serving:

1 teaspoon confection-
  ers' sugar
1 tablespoon butter
sprinkle of grated nut-
  meg
1 jigger (1½ ounces)
  rum
boiling water

Place all ingredients except the boiling water in a mug (not the large ones). When ready to serve, pour water almost to top.

Cheddar Fondue Cubes

These can be picked up with your fingers because they will not drip. You want the cubes to be about the size of a large marshmallow. Very easy to make and they freeze well. Makes approximately 8 dozen appetizers.

1 long loaf (approxi-
  mately 1 pound) un-
  sliced French bread,
  1 to 2 days old
½ cup butter
1 large (8-ounce) pack-
  age cream cheese
½ pound sharp Ched-
  dar cheese, shredded
¼ teaspoon garlic
  powder
2 egg whites, stiffly
  beaten

Cut the untrimmed bread into cubes about ¾ inch square. Melt butter and cream cheese over gently boiling water in the top of a double boiler. Gradually add the shredded cheese, stirring until melted and smooth. Stir in the garlic powder. Remove from heat and quickly fold in the beaten egg whites. Keeping the top of double boiler over the hot water, use 2 forks (fondue forks work well) to dip cubes quickly in the cheese, coating them evenly. Tap fork lightly, then place cubes slightly apart on greased baking sheet. If cheese becomes too thick to coat the last cubes, place double boiler over heat just to warm cheese. Let coated cubes stand, uncovered, until dry to the touch, about 2½ hours. If desired, freeze until firm, then package airtight. To serve, place desired number of cubes on ungreased baking sheet. Bake at 350° for 6-8 minutes (10-12 minutes if frozen).

Creamed Chipped Beef in Patty Shells

This tasty dish came from my neighbor, who is a superb hostess and cook. It is a good recipe for a large number of people and is also good on Holland Rusks. Serves 6 (triple quantities for 18 people).

1 package frozen patty shells
¼ pound chipped beef, cut in strips
¼ cup butter
½ onion, minced
3 tablespoons flour
1 cup milk
1 cup sour cream
1 cup shredded Cheddar cheese
1 can (4 ounces) sliced mushrooms
2 tablespoons minced parsley
salt and pepper to taste

Bake patty shells according to package directions. Sauté beef and onion in melted butter until onion is translucent. Blend in flour; add milk, stirring constantly until sauce is smooth and thickened. Add rest of ingredients, stirring constantly until very hot. Spoon into patty shells.

Orange Sherbet Salad Mold

This is very light, refreshing and delicious and easy to make. Serve this on a pretty dish with lettuce and watercress. Serves 10. (double quantitites for 18 people).

1 large (6-ounce) package orange gelatin
1 small (3-ounce) package lemon gelatin
2 cups boiling water
½ cup orange juice
1 quart orange sherbet
1 can (11 ounces) mandarin oranges, drained

Dissolve gelatin in water. Add orange juice, beat in sherbet with wire whisk. Refrigerate until partially set. Pour over oranges arranged in bottom of 6-cup mold; chill until firm.

Crudités

Cut up lots of raw vegetables and refrigerate in serving dish with ice cubes to keep them crisp. These will look nice on your table and will go well with the Chipped Beef.

Date Nut Bread

This is especially good and easy. Recipe is for one loaf (make 2 for 18 people).

2 tablespoons butter
¾ cup boiling water
½ cup sugar
1 cup pitted dates, chopped
1¾ cup sifted flour
1 teaspoon soda
½ teaspoon salt
1 egg
½ cup chopped walnuts or pecans

Melt butter in boiling water. Add sugar and dates. Set aside to cool. Combine flour, soda and salt. Add beaten egg to cooled date mixture. Then add flour mixture, then nuts. Bake at 350° for 40-50 minutes in a greased and floured loaf pan. Cool before slicing.

Fudge Ring

You and your guests cannot help but love this. Freezes well. Serve it on a white doily on a pretty china or glass dish. Cut a few ½-inch slices and let the guests cut their own if you wish. If you cut them, you will get 36 ½-inch slices!

1 small (6-ounce) package semisweet chocolate morsels
1 small (6-ounce) package butterscotch morsels
1 can sweetened condensed milk
1 cup coarsely chopped walnuts
½ teaspoon vanilla
1 cup walnut halves for garnish

Melt chocolate and butterscotch morsels with sweetened condensed milk in top of double boiler over hot water. Stir occasionally until morsels melt and mixture begins to thicken. Remove from heat; add chopped walnuts and vanilla. Blend well. Chill for 1 hour until mixture thickens. Line bottom of 9-inch pie pan with a 12-inch square of foil. Place ¾ cup walnut halves in bottom of pan, forming 2-inch wide flat ring. Spoon chocolate mixture in small mounds on top of walnuts to form ring. Decorate with remaining walnuts. (Will look like a coffee cake ring.) Chill in refrigerator until firm enough to slice.

FEBRUARY

MIDWINTER BLUES FESTIVE BRUNCH
Serves 6

Champagne Cocktail
Celebration Ham*
Luscious Scalloped Oysters*
Tomato-Lemon Aspic*
Baked Fruit With Sour Cream*
Coffee Cake Exceptionale**
Coffee

There is no better cure for the February blahs than a scrumptious brunch. Your guests will love the idea, and you will enjoy preparing and serving this delicious menu. From the subtle flavor of the scalloped oysters to the rich combination of baked fruit, the whole menu is very special. Have your guests seated at the table as soon as they all arrive and serve the champagne immediately.

Table Setting

For this formal brunch, use a white organdy cloth over a pastel sheet. A silver bowl holding a mixed bouquet from the florist will add to your traditional table setting. Use your finest crystal, china, silver and your silver serving dishes. The pastel linen napkins should match the under-cloth. Flowered china place card holders will add the final touch of formality to this very elegant brunch.

*Do ahead
**Freeze

Champagne Cocktail

A lovely drink for any special occasion. Makes 1 serving.

1 sugar cube
dash aromatic bitters
1 lemon twist
champagne, chilled

Place sugar in champagne glass; add bitters and lemon twist. Slowly pour in champagne to fill glass.

Celebration Ham

You may wish to use ½ a ham for only 6 persons. However, it will always be enjoyed at a later date, so do not worry about leftovers.

**1 hickory-smoked,
   sugar-cured ham
1 cup sherry
1½ cups brown sugar
2 tablespoons mustard**

Scrub ham with clean brush; trim to remove mold. Cover with water; add ½ cup sherry. Soak overnight. Place ham in long roaster, fat-side-up; add ½ cup water and remaining sherry. Cover tightly. Bake at 325° for 15 minutes per pound. Remove cover for the last 45 minutes of baking time. Skin ham and score. Combine brown sugar and mustard; glaze ham with mixture. Cool to room temperature; slice thinly to serve.

Luscious Scalloped Oysters

This really is delicious. Serves 8.

**2 quarts raw oysters
10 slices bread
1 cup butter**

Sauce:

**½ cup oyster liquid
½ cup heavy cream
1 teaspoon salt
dash of pepper
1 teaspoon Worcester-
   shire sauce**

Toast bread until quite dry and golden brown. With kitchen scissors snip the toast into very small uneven pieces (about ¾ × ¼ inches). Melt the butter and toss the toast pieces in the melted butter until well coated. Place oysters in strainer over bowl. Save the juice. In a heavy, shallow baking dish arrange ⅓ of toast pieces, then place ½ of the oysters over toast. Arrange another ⅓ toast and cover with remainder of oysters. Pour the combined sauce ingredients over all, then arrange last ⅓ of the toast bits over top. Some oysters will show through. Never have more than 2 layers of oysters. Bake at 425° for 30 minutes. After it comes out of the oven you may wish to pour ½ cup heavy cream over top (optional).

Tomato-Lemon Aspic

This is a wonderful addition to any meal. Easy to make. Serves 6-8.

**1 large (6-ounce) pack-
   age lemon gelatin
2½ cups hot water
2 cans tomato sauce
1½ tablespoons
   vinegar**

**½ teaspoon salt
dash pepper**

Dissolve gelatin in hot water. Add rest of ingredients and mix. Pour into mold and refrigerate.

Baked Fruit With Sour Cream

This has been in our family for years and has been everyone's favorite. A good time to prepare this is an hour before guests come. Let it sit on your counter after it has been cooked. Easily prepared. Serves 6-8.

1 large can peach
   halves
1 large can apricot
   halves
1 large can pear halves
1 large can pitted bing
   cherries
2 boxes frozen straw-
   berries, slightly
   thawed
1 cup dark brown
   sugar

½ cup fruit juice
½ cup rum
sour cream

Drain first four fruits; save ½ cup juice. Arrange first four fruits in a casserole. Lay the contents of the boxes of frozen strawberries in the middle, side by side. Sprinkle fruits with sugar, add juice and rum. Bake at 350° for 35 minutes. Serve warm, topped with sour cream.

Coffee Cake Exceptionale

Easily made and tastes extra good. Freezes well. About 14 servings.

¾ cup butter
1½ cups sugar
3 eggs
1½ teaspoons vanilla
3 cups flour
1½ teaspoons baking
   powder
1½ teaspoons soda
¼ teaspoon salt
1½ cups dairy cream

Filling:

½ cup brown sugar,
   packed
½ cup finely chopped
   nuts
1½ teaspoons cinna-
   mon

Heat oven to 350°. Grease 10x4-inch tube pan, 12-cup bundt pan or 2 loaf pans. Combine butter, sugar, eggs and vanilla in a large mixing bowl. Beat 2 minutes. Mix in flour, baking powder, soda and salt alternately with sour cream. For tube or bundt pan, spread ⅓ of batter in pan and sprinkle with ⅓ of filling; repeat twice.

For loaf pans, spread ¼ of batter in each pan and sprinkle each with ¼ of filling; repeat. Bake 1 hour or until wooden toothpick inserted comes out clean. Cool slightly in pan before removing.

MARDI GRAS PANCAKE BRUNCH
Serves 8

> **Spiced Coffee with Floating Oranges**
> **Stuffed Grapefruit***
> **Silver Dollar Pancakes**
> **Apple-Sausage Ring***
> **Frozen Coffee Tortonis****
> **Coffee and Tea**

Mardi Gras is a gay tradition that should not be thought of as an exclusive New Orleans celebration. People all over the country can enjoy the festivities that come with the Carnival season. This is a perfect time to invite good friends for a pancake brunch and to listen to your collection of jazz records. A heavy soup tureen for the Spiced Coffee will look especially nice with clove-studded oranges floating on top. Serve this in pre-warmed glass root beer mugs in the room where you will be listening to music. The stuffed grapefruit is unusually attractive and delicious. Your guests will enjoy choosing between Vermont maple syrup and fruit toppings for their pancakes and they will certainly ask for the Apple-Sausage Ring recipe. As an ending to this hearty brunch, the Frozen Coffee Tortoni is light and refreshing.

Table Setting

To go along with your casual mood and winter brunch menu, a red and white checkered cloth will be fun to use. A pewter bowl in the center of the table filled with red and white carnations will look perky. Use stainless flatware and red napkins. If you have any red glass plates and water goblets, use them, as they will really look terrific.

*Do ahead
**Freeze

Spiced Coffee With Floating Oranges
Very good and very pretty. Makes 8 ½-cup servings.

4 cups water
2 tablespoons brown sugar
4 3-inch cinnamon sticks
2 oranges, peel only
½ teaspoon whole allspice
2 tablespoons instant coffee
3 whole oranges
whole cloves

Floating oranges: Heat oven to 325°. Insert whole cloves about ½ inch apart in 3 oranges. Place in baking pan with just enough water to cover bottom of pan. Bake 30 minutes uncovered. These can be baked a day ahead, covered and refrigerated until ready to serve.
Coffee: In saucepan, combine all ingredients except coffee; heat to boiling. Strain; pour liquid over coffee in heat-proof container. Stir until coffee is dissolved. Float oranges in coffee.

Stuffed Grapefruit

Serve these in a thick bed of parsley in a glass cereal dish and you will have a delicious looking and tasty treat. Serves 8.

4 large grapefruit
2 pounds small shrimp, shelled and deveined
1 pound mushrooms, sliced
1½ teaspoons lemon juice
1½ teaspoons salt
1 cup mayonnaise

Cut grapefruit in half, cutting edges into a sawtooth design. Remove seeds. Insert small knife blade between white inner skin and meat of grapefruit. Cut completely around grapefruit with sawing motion, freeing meat from shell. Cut down on each side of grapefruit segment to free meat from membranes. Cut core at base and remove with membranes attached. Reserve segments and as much juice as possible. Put shrimp, mushrooms, grapefruit juice, lemon juice and salt in a saucepan; cover. Bring to a boil and cook 2 minutes. Remove from heat and let cool in liquid. Combine mayonnaise, cooking liquid, shrimp, mushrooms and grapefruit segments. Mix gently. Spoon into grapefruit shells. Refrigerate and serve cold.

Silver Dollar Pancakes

The canned milk makes a significant difference in lightness.

2 cups flour
2 tablespoons sugar
2 tablespoons baking powder
½ teaspoon salt

2 eggs
1½ cups canned evaporated milk
1 cup water
1½ tablespoons melted butter

Beat eggs, milk and water and add to mixed dry ingredients. Whip well, adding butter. Pour enough batter on the griddle to cover a silver dollar. Keep adding to a heat-proof platter in a low-set oven. Serve with melted butter, real Vermont maple syrup and various fruit toppings.

Apple-Sausage Ring

This can easily be done ahead. It is a favorite in our household. Serves 8.

2 pounds bulk sausage
2 eggs, slightly beaten
½ cup milk
1½ cups cracker crumbs or herbed stuffing
¼ cup minced onion
1 cup finely chopped apples

Combine all ingredients and mix thoroughly. Press lightly into a greased 6-cup ring mold. Turn out onto a shallow baking pan. Bake at 350° for 1 hour. Drain. You can make this the day before and partially bake for 30 minutes. Finish baking before serving.

Frozen Coffee Tortonis

Very light, refreshing and delicious and easy to make. Your guests will be most impressed! Serves 8.

1 egg white
1 teaspoon instant coffee
2 tablespoons sugar
1 cup heavy cream
1 teaspoon vanilla
½ teaspoon almond extract
2 tablespoons chopped almonds, toasted
2 tablespoons coconut, toasted

Whip egg white until stiff, then add coffee, sugar, ½ of the nuts and ½ of the coconut. Whip cream, add vanilla and almond extract. Fold beaten whites into whipped cream. Pour into paper cups and top with remaining nuts and coconut. Freeze. This should be removed from freezer about 15 minutes before serving; however, once it begins to thaw, it melts quickly.

ST. VALENTINE'S DAY BRUNCH
Serves 10

Cranberry Punch*

Cinnamon Sticks**

**Chicken Livers With Grapes
on Toast Points***

Baked Eggs and Spinach Casserole

Tasty Puffs*

**Coeur à la Crème
with Strawberry Sauce***

Coffee

Valentine's Day is a sentimental time, so why not invite really good friends for brunch? Start your entertaining by serving a cup of Cranberry Punch and specially cut heart-shaped cinnamon sticks. Something that is fun to do and very appropriate for Valentine's Day parties is to pick partners and seating arrangements by chance. Prepare a lacy valentine for each couple and cut each in half (haphazardly) and put the halves in separate boxes. Let the men draw from one box and the women from the other as they arrive. They must find the corresponding half by the time brunch is served. The couples whose valentines match will be partners for the meal. The heart-shaped Coeur à la Crème will be a fitting and romantic end for your Valentine's Day brunch.

Table Setting

Pink is the color for Valentine's Day. Use it lavishly! Pink tablecloth and napkins should be used. A cut-glass bowl on the table, holding pink sweetheart roses and babies' breath and surrounded by crystal birds, will make an appropriate centerpiece. Pastel flowered china with sterling silver flatware will add elegance to your buffet table.

*Do ahead
**Freeze

Cranberry Punch

Something pink-red for the occasion. Makes 10 servings.

½ cup sugar
1 cup water
½ teaspoon whole
  cloves
3 cinnamon sticks
2 cups cranberry juice
½ cup lemon juice
1 cup orange juice

3 cups ginger ale
1 fifth rum

Mix first four ingredients; boil 5 minutes. Strain; cool. Mix with fruit juices. Refrigerate. Just before serving, pour into a punch bowl over an ice ring. Add ginger ale and rum.

Cinnamon Sticks

My sister in Atlanta, who has a reputation as a great cook, serves these often and receives requests for this recipe all the time. They are perfect for a coffee, tea or any occasion. Make plenty and just watch how quickly they disappear! Use a heart-shaped cookie cutter for Valentine's Day! Prepare, freeze and then cook. Makes approximately 36 sticks.

1 loaf firm-textured
  white bread, un-
  sliced or sliced
2 sticks butter, melted
⅓ cup cinnamon
1 cup sugar

Decrust bread and cut into ¾-inch slices, then into ¾-inch strips. (Packaged sliced bread can be used and then cut into ¾-inch strips.) Dip the strips in melted butter and place on a rack. Sprinkle generously with combined cinnamon and sugar on all sides. (Can be packaged and frozen at this point.) Bake at 400° for 8 minutes on a cookie sheet. Good hot or cooled. (Optional — the strips may be sprinkled with rum.)

Chicken Livers With Grapes and Toast Points

This will look very tempting, surrounded by many toast points on a pretty, warmed pewter or china serving dish. Prepare before your guests arrive and keep on low heat in top of a double boiler. Serves 10.

2½ pounds chicken
  livers
5 tablespoons minced
  green onions
10 tablespoons (1 stick
  plus 2 tablespoons)
  butter
flour
½ teaspoon salt
¼ teaspoon ginger

¼ teaspoon pepper
2 teaspoons Worcester-
  shire sauce
3½ cups seedless
  grapes
½ cup sherry
¾ cup chicken broth
½ cup sour cream
chopped parsley

Dry livers with paper towels. Dust with flour. Heat butter in large skillet over medium-high heat. Add onions and livers; brown about 7 minutes. Add salt, ginger, pepper, Worcestershire sauce, grapes, sherry and chicken broth. Reduce heat, cover and cook 5 minutes. Blend in sour cream, stirring gently, over low heat. Turn into serving dish. Sprinkle with parsley. Arrange toast points around livers.

Baked Eggs and Spinach Casserole

Have everything done separately and put together just as it goes into the oven before your guests arrive. This will look very pretty and goes well with the chicken livers and toast points. Serves 10.

5 packages (10 ounces each) frozen chopped spinach, thawed and drained
salt
8 tablespoons (1 stick) butter
8 tablespoons flour
2½ cups milk
2½ cups shredded Cheddar cheese
10 eggs
pepper

Preheat oven to 325°. In a 13x9-inch baking dish, arrange spinach in an even layer and add 1 teaspoon salt. With spoon, make 10 indentations in spinach. In medium saucepan over low heat, melt butter. Add flour and stir until smooth. Gradually stir in milk and cook, stirring constantly until sauce is thickened. Stir in cheese and heat just until cheese is melted. Break one egg into each indentation. Sprinkle eggs with pepper and ¼ teaspoon salt. Pour sauce over eggs. Bake 30-35 minutes until eggs are set.

Tasty Puffs

These are light and delicious. Make ahead of your meal and reheat. Makes 15 puffs.

⅓ cup shortening
½ cup sugar
1 egg
1½ cups flour
1½ teaspoons baking powder
½ teaspoon salt
¼ teaspoon nutmeg
½ cup milk
½ cup sugar

1 teaspoon cinnamon
½ cup butter, melted

Preheat oven to 350°. Grease 15 medium muffin cups. Mix shortening, ½ cup sugar and the egg. Stir in flour, baking powder, salt and nutmeg alternately with milk. Fill muffin cups ⅔ full. Bake 20-25 minutes. Mix ½ cup sugar and the cinnamon. Roll hot puffs in melted butter, then in cinnamon-sugar.

Coeur à la Crème with Strawberry Sauce

You will need a heart-shaped basket for this, or individual porcelain heart-shaped molds. A large department store or a gourmet shop usually carries both. Your guests will be very impressed with the appearance and the taste. Easy to prepare. Serves 10.

½ pound cream cheese, softened
½ cup confectioners' sugar
salt
½ vanilla bean
2 cups heavy cream
cheesecloth

Sauce:

¼ cup dry sherry
¾ cup red currant jelly
1½ cups sliced strawberries (preferably fresh)
1 tablespoon lemon juice

Beat cream cheese in electric mixer until light and fluffy. Slowly add confectioners' sugar and pinch of salt. With a sharp small knife, cut ½ vanilla bean lengthwise, scrape seeds into mixture; stir well. In metal bowl set in ice, add cream and beat until cream holds form when dropped from end of whisk. Add cheese mixture and whisk until ingredients are well mixed. Wring out cheesecloth in ice water. Use to line basket mold. Refrigerate for at least 6 hours, putting mold on a plate in case it drains some.

Sauce: Add sherry and currant jelly to a saucepan over low heat. Stir until melted. Cool. Add strawberries and lemon juice. Chill.

You can either unmold the heart in the kitchen on a pretty platter or unmold it in front of your guests. Spoon onto dessert dishes and pour some sauce on top.

MARCH

FAMILY ENGAGEMENT PARTY BRUNCH
Serves 6

Champagne
Oyster And Bacon Roll-Ups*
Strawberry Cubes Elegante*
Crepes Suzette*
Broccoli And Egg Casserole*
Crunchy Ice Cream Pie**
Coffee and Tea

Your daughter has become engaged. Getting to know the parents of the prospective groom is a happy task for you. Invite them to brunch along with the newly engaged couple. You will have lots to talk about and a brunch party can stretch to late afternoon. This way there will be plenty of time to make plans as well as to get to know the other parents better. A relationship could not get off to a better start than with Champagne and Oyster and Bacon Roll-Ups followed by a parade of elegant foods. The Strawberry Cubes Elegante will earn many compliments, as they are lovely to look at and quite different. Pick your favorite flavor to fill the ice cream pie; this is an easy but very delicious way to end your brunch.

Table Setting

For this occasion you will want to use your dining room for a sit-down meal. Show off the beautiful wood of your table by using heavy white placemats instead of a tablecloth. A white ceramic basket filled with greens and pink flowers will be a delicate touch on your table. Make two bows of 3-inch wide green and white checked gingham — each should be 4 feet long to start and should have long streamers when completed. Place one bow on each side of the basket so that the streamers lie gracefully lengthwise on the table. Roll three pink and three green napkins, tying them with narrow gingham ribbon — pink and white for the green napkins and green and white ribbon for the pink napkins. Alternate these on the table for a surprisingly attractive look. Use your best china, crystal and silver for this special occasion.

*Do ahead
**Freeze

Champagne

A perfect drink for a celebration. Buy a bottle or two of good Champagne and chill. Make it perfect by using champagne glasses and use your champagne cooler if you have one.

Oyster and Bacon Roll-Ups

These delicious morsels are also known as "angels on horseback." They are easy to prepare. Make about 3 per person.

1½ dozen fresh oysters, shucked
bacon
toothpicks

Cut strips of bacon in half crosswise. Wrap each half around one oyster. Secure with a toothpick. Broil about 5 minutes turning once. Serve hot.

Strawberry Cubes Elegante

This really does look lovely and tastes delicious. Serves 6.

1 envelope unflavored gelatin (1 tablespoon)
½ cup Rhine wine
¼ cup sugar
1¼ cups Rhine wine
1 pint strawberries, halved and sweetened

Sprinkle gelatin over ½ cup wine in saucepan. Place over low heat and stir constantly until dissolved (about 3 minutes). Remove from heat and add sugar and 1¼ cups wine. Stir until clear. Pour into 9 × 5-inch loaf pan. Chill until firm. Cut into cubes. Layer in parfait glasses with strawberries and chill until ready to serve.

Crepes Suzette

These are actually quite easy to prepare. The flavor is fantastic and cannot help but impress everyone. Serves 6-8.

6 eggs, well beaten
4 tablespoons flour
½ teaspoon salt
2 tablespoons milk
2 tablespoons water
2 teaspoons grated orange rind

Sauce:
6 tablespoons butter
1 cup sugar
⅔ cup orange juice
1 teaspoon grated orange rind
curaçao

Combine ingredients for crepes and beat well. Bake in thin cakes on hot greased griddle, browning both sides. Make sauce by creaming butter and sugar together, beating orange juice and rind in gradually. Spread on cakes as they are baked and roll up quickly. (If preferred, fold crepes in quarters.) To serve, pour curaçao over crepes and ignite; turn crepes over as blazing continues. Serve as soon as flame goes out. Serve with additional sauce.

Broccoli and Egg Casserole

This is a little more than a vegetable and is easily prepared. Serves 6.

3 packages (10 ounces
  each) frozen
  chopped broccoli,
  cooked and drained
3 hard-cooked eggs,
  peeled and sliced
1½ cups sour cream
¾ cup mayonnaise
3 tablespoons tarragon
  vinegar
¼ teaspoon paprika

Preheat oven to 350°. Arrange broccoli in an ungreased shallow 2-quart casserole, top with egg slices and set aside. Over lowest heat, warm sour cream with mayonnaise and vinegar, stirring 4-5 minutes (do not boil); pour over broccoli. Bake, uncovered, 10 minutes; sprinkle with paprika and serve.

Crunchy Ice Cream Pie

This is a surprise pie! Few can guess the crust; however, it is a favorite for any age and is easy to make. Serves 6-8.

3 tablespoons butter
1 package (6 ounces)
  chocolate chips
2 cups Rice Krispies
1 quart peppermint
  stick, chocolate chip
  mint, or your favor-
  ite flavor ice cream

In a saucepan melt the butter and chocolate chips. Stir in the Rice Krispies and remove from the heat. With a fork, mash until the consistency of graham cracker crust. Line a 9-inch pie plate or 9-inch springform pan with mixture. Freeze. Partially thaw ice cream and fill pie shell. Freeze until ready to serve.

IMPORTANT PERSON BRUNCH
Serves 6

Café Cappuccino

Melon Rings
with Fresh and Frozen Fruit*

Salmon à la Newburg in Croustades*

Buttered Peas

Artichoke Grapefruit Salad*

Sesame Straws*

Apricot Mousse*

Your civic committee has invited a local female author to speak at a 9 o'clock meeting and you, as chairman, would like to entertain her and officers of the club. This is a perfect time for a brunch, as the meeting will end in the morning. This entire menu is perfect for a ladies' brunch, as each item is light and pleasing to the eye. Graceful china coffee mugs will add to the flavor of your Café Cappuccino served before brunch.

Table Setting

Now that March is here, you can really start thinking about spring. A grass-green linen tablecloth with matching napkins sets the stage for your centerpiece. In anticipation of spring, I always plant some paper narcissus bulbs in a bed of white stones and water. They look best in a fluted flowered china quiche dish. By March they are blooming prettily and will remind your guests that spring is around the corner. Luncheon plates with flower or herb designs will help carry out your spring theme.

*Do ahead
**Freeze

Café Cappuccino

A pleasant change from regular coffee and a special treat. Makes 6 servings.

2 cups boiling water
3 tablespoons freeze-
   dried espresso coffee
2 cups scalded milk
ground nutmeg
6 cinnamon sticks (op-
   tional)

Pour boiling water, coffee, then hot milk into blender. Turn to high until frothy. Pour into cups and dust with nutmeg. May be served with a cinnamon stick.

Melon Rings with Fresh and Frozen Fruit

Serve this on a glass dessert plate or a flat soup dish. Any fruit will do. If you have frozen peaches or other fruits, just take a handful and place on each melon ring early in morning. Serves 6.

2 cantaloupes
2 bananas
2 cups frozen blueber-
  ries, thawed
2 small boxes frozen
  raspberries, thawed

Cut melons crosswise into 5 slices each; discard ends and use 3 center rings from each melon. Remove seeds. Place one ring flat into each dish. Divide fruit onto 6 dishes and top with raspberries.

Salmon à la Newburg in Croustades

This looks harder than it really is, but it is well worth the time. You can do this ahead of time and reheat in a double boiler. Serves 6.

1 pound can salmon
¼ pound fresh mush-
  rooms
5 tablespoons butter
1½ tablespoons flour
1 cup milk
½ cup heavy cream
2 egg yolks
½ teaspoon Worcester-
  shire sauce
1 teaspoon lemon juice
3 tablespoons sherry

Drain salmon; remove skin and bones; flake the fish. Slice mushrooms and sauté until golden brown in 1 tablespoon butter. Melt remaining 4 tablespoons butter in a double boiler. Add flour and blend; add milk and cream, gradually stirring until smooth and thickened. Beat egg yolks slightly and pour white sauce over them, stirring constantly. Add seasonings and blend. Add mushrooms and salmon and heat until salmon is hot, stirring carefully.

Croustades:
1 loaf unsliced white
  bread
butter

Croustades: Preheat oven to 375°. Trim crusts from bread; cut loaf into 2-inch thick slices. Cut slices into squares or oblongs. With fingers, pull out center of each, leaving ¼-⅜-inch thick shell. Brush with melted butter, place on cookie sheet; bake 12-15 minutes until golden. Fill each croustade with some of the Salmon à la Newburg.

Buttered Peas

Buy a large bag of frozen peas. Add a little water and bring to a boil. Turn heat off and let sit for a few minutes. Drain, add butter, salt, pepper and serve!

Artichoke Grapefruit Salad

A little different and very nice. Serves 6.

1 can (15-ounces) artichoke hearts, drained
¼ cup salad oil
2 tablespoons vinegar
1 teaspoon Worcestershire sauce
¼ teaspoon salt
⅛ teaspoon pepper
1 tablespoon parsley
3 cups iceberg lettuce
2 cups romaine
1 cup endive
2 pink grapefruits, sectioned

Cut artichokes in half; combine oil, vinegar, Worcestershire sauce, salt, pepper, parsley and mix. Pour over artichokes in a bowl and chill for 3 or 4 hours. Combine cut-up greens in a large bowl. Add artichoke mixture, grapefruit sections and toss lightly.

Sesame Sticks

These are very easy to make and can be done ahead of time. Securely wrap in aluminum foil and reheat at 375° for 8 minutes. Makes 35 sticks.

1 package (8 ounces) refrigerated crescent rolls
melted butter
sesame seeds

Unroll dough. Pinch seams together. Cut each section into strips. Place on ungreased cookie sheet. Brush generously with melted butter and sprinkle with sesame seeds. Bake at 375° for 10 minutes or until puffy, golden brown and crispy.

Apricot Mousse

Really light, refreshing and delicious and easy to prepare. Serves 6.

1 large (1-pound, 14-ounce) can apricots
1 package lemon gelatin
1 teaspoon vanilla
3 tablespoons apricot brandy or Cointreau
1 cup heavy cream, whipped
1 package ladyfingers, split

Drain apricots (reserving liquid) and puree in blender. Heat reserved liquid plus enough water to measure 1¾ cups to the boiling point. Remove from heat and add gelatin, stirring until dissolved. Add pureed apricots, vanilla and brandy, then chill until it begins to thicken. Beat slightly and fold in whipped cream. Line a crystal bowl with ladyfingers and pour in mousse. Refrigerate.

ST. PATRICK'S DAY BRUNCH
Serves 14

Irish Coffee

Irish Oatmeal Bread With Sweet Butter**

Puffy Batter-Dipped Toast
(with Maple Syrup)

Sausage-Stuffed Apples*

Lime-Pear Gelatin Mold*

Frozen Grasshopper Surprise**

Coffee

Whether you are Irish or wish you were, St. Patrick's Day belongs to all of us. The gay mood which characterizes this day's festivities is the key to a successful brunch. This will make the holiday seem longer, whether you entertain on St. Patrick's Day morning or on the preceding weekend. Irish Coffee is always a big hit and will be perfect to start off this brunch. Irish Oatmeal Bread, which is typically Irish in its delicious nut-like flavor, is also a perfect complement to the meal. The emerald-green color of the Pear-Lime Gelatin Mold will add a colorful note to your table. The food can be used on many occasions, but goes together well for this special day. You will find the Frozen Grasshopper Surprise will be popular winter, spring, summer or fall and will be a great end to a truly memorable party.

Table Setting

If you have any Irish in you, let it come out in your decorations! Use a white tablecloth on your buffet table, with a crystal bowl of green carnations in the center. Set the bowl down on a frill made of green crepe paper. Coming out beneath the bowl should be as many narrow green ribbons as you have guests. Each ribbon runs to a tiny pot of live shamrocks for a favor that can be taken home after brunch. You can add a green flag with a guest's name on each plant. White napkins rolled and tied with shiny Kelly green paper ribbons curled on the ends and glass plates will create a festive atmosphere for your Irish brunch.

*Do ahead
**Freeze

Irish Coffee

This is the greatest. Use regular Irish Coffee glasses or some pretty mugs with handles. Makes 1 serving.

1½ teaspoons sugar
1 jigger Irish whisky
hot strong black coffee
whipped cream

Into a glass or coffee mug, measure sugar and Irish whisky; add hot coffee to within ½-inch of top. Stir to dissolve sugar. Top with whipped cream. Do not stir. Sip coffee through cream.

Irish Oatmeal Bread with Sweet Butter

This smells great while cooking and tastes even better. Make this and freeze; wrap securely in aluminum foil and reheat in oven. Have a tub of sweet butter on your serving table or spread it on ahead of time. Easily prepared. Makes 2 loaves.

3 cups sifted flour
1¼ cups quick-cooking
   rolled oats
1½ tablespoons baking
   powder
1 tablespoon salt
½ cup honey
1½ cups milk
1 tablespoon melted
   butter
1 egg, beaten

Preheat oven to 350°. Mix first 4 ingredients. In another bowl add honey, milk and butter to the beaten egg. Pour egg mixture into oat mixture, stirring until dry ingredients are moistened. Mixture will be lumpy. Spread into 2 greased and floured loaf pans. Bake 1 hour. Turn out of pans onto a wire rack. Brush with more melted butter while warm.

Puffy Batter-Dipped Toast (with Maple Syrup)

This is like a French toast. You can make it a little ahead of serving and keep on low in your oven. Serve with maple syrup. Serves 20. Allow approximately 1½ slices per person.

1 cup pancake mix
½ teaspoon cinnamon
⅛ teaspoon nutmeg
20 slices firm bread
powdered sugar
maple syrup

Mix pancake batter according to directions on box of mix, and add cinnamon and nutmeg. Dip bread into batter and then deep fry until golden brown. Dust with powdered sugar. Serve hot with maple syrup.

Sausage-Stuffed Apples

Your guests will like this easily prepared extra touch. Serves 14.

14 baking apples
2 pounds pork sausage meat
14 fresh mushrooms

Wash and core apples, and pare upper ¼ of each. Place in casserole. Stem mushrooms. Slice stems and mix with sausage meat. Fill cores of apples with mixture and top with mushroom caps. Bake at 350° for 35 minutes.

Lime-Pear Gelatin Mold

Looks lovely and tastes very nice. Serves 7 (double for 14).

1 can (1 pound) pear halves (7)
1 small (3-ounce) package lime gelatin
2 tablespoons lemon juice
½ cup crumbled blue cheese
1 cup creamed cottage cheese
paprika
½ cup finely chopped red-skinned apple
½ cup mayonnaise

Drain pears well and add enough water to syrup to make 1¾ cups. Heat liquid and pour over gelatin, stirring until dissolved. Add lemon juice and cool. Pour small amount (about ½-inch deep) into 8-inch cake pan. Chill until set. Meanwhile, combine blue cheese with 2 tablespoons cottage cheese and blend well. Divide mixture evenly into hollows of pear halves. Sprinkle with paprika and arrange, cheese-side-down, in gelatin (6 in a circle and 1 in center). Fold remaining cottage cheese, apple and mayonnaise into remaining gelatin. Pour over pears and chill until firm. Unmold on greens.

Frozen Grasshopper Surprise

This was served at a ladies' church luncheon for 150. Very easy. One hint: serve right from the freezer. You will certainly use this recipe many times. Double this recipe for 14 people. Serves 8.

24 Oreo cookies
¼ cup melted butter
2 cups heavy cream, whipped
¼ cup crème de menthe (green)
1 jar (7 ounces) marshmallow fluff

Place cookies in a blender and spin until all are crumbled. Combine with melted butter. Line a 9-inch springform pan with cookie mixture, saving ¼ cup for trim. Mix together rest of ingredients. Pour into pan and top with remaining crumbs. Freeze. When firm, remove from pan and wrap in aluminum foil and stick back in freezer. Ready to serve!

APRIL

BIRTHDAY BRUNCH FOR YOUR HUSBAND

Serves 6

> **Open Bar**
> **Fresh Fruit Compote***
> **Scrambled Eggs and Mushrooms**
> **French Toast Special**
> **Little Sausages and Apple Rings**
> **Heavenly Pie***
> **Coffee**

Why not invite your husband's best and dearest friends and their wives for a special birthday brunch? A daytime party will give everyone lots of time to chat and enjoy each other and will be good if your guests have to travel any distance. So that your husband and his friends can drink what they enjoy best, an open bar is a good idea. It might also be a good idea to mix up a batch of Bloody Marys for the gals to enjoy. This is a hearty menu that men will love. Instead of the traditional birthday cake, make your husband's favorite dessert — one thing that is a favorite around our house is the Heavenly Pie.

Table Setting

For this man's brunch, use a dark plaid sheet (double-bed size) with napkins in a complementary color. Make a bed of rhododendron branches in the center of your table and nestle a wooden duck decoy in them. Stark white china and plain silver will complete this casually elegant setting.

*Do ahead
**Freeze

Fresh Fruit Compote

An interesting fruit combination. Serves 6-8.

3 navel oranges
3 ripe bananas
1 fresh pineapple
1 pint strawberries
½ cup brown sugar,
  sifted
1 ounce kirsch
1 cup sour cream

Peel 2 oranges, removing all membranes; section. Squeeze juice from other orange and reserve. Slice bananas thin; peel and cube pineapple; hull, wash and slice strawberries. Place all fruits in serving bowl, sprinkle with sugar, pour orange juice over all. Chill at least 2 hours. Just before serving, stir in kirsch; mound sour cream in center of fruit.

Scrambled Eggs and Mushrooms

These really delicious eggs can be made a little in advance and kept warm by following the directions below. Serves 6.

1 dozen eggs
½ cup light cream
1 teaspoon salt
¼ teaspoon pepper
1½ tablespoons butter

Sauce:

2 tablespoons butter
2 tablespoons flour
¼ teaspoon salt
⅛ teaspoon pepper
1 cup milk
parsley
1 can (3 or 4 ounces)
  sliced mushrooms,
  drained.

Crack eggs into a bowl and add light cream, salt and pepper; beat until blended. Melt butter in a large frying pan and pour in the egg mixture. Cook slowly, stirring occasionally, until almost set. Fold sauce into eggs while they are still creamy. Keep the mixture hot in an electric frying pan set at the lowest heat, or in a very slow oven (200°), or over boiling water in the top of a chafing dish. Sprinkle with parsley and garnish the top with sliced mushrooms.

Sauce: Melt butter over low heat in a saucepan. Blend in flour and seasonings. Cook over low heat, stirring until mixture is smooth and bubbly. Remove from heat. Stir in milk. Bring to boil, stirring constantly. Boil 1 minute.

French Toast Special

Serve real maple syrup with this. A little more work than regular French toast but well worth the time. Serves 6.

1 loaf day-old unsliced
  homemade-type or
  firm-textured bread
2 cups light cream

8 eggs, well beaten
½ teaspoon salt
vegetable oil
confectioners' sugar

Cut 6 slices of bread ¾-inch thick. Trim and cut into two triangles. Combine cream with eggs and salt. Dip triangles into mixture, letting them absorb as much as possible. Fry in ½-inch hot vegetable oil in electric frying pan set at 325°, turning once until golden brown. Put triangles in shallow baking pan and bake in 400° oven 3-5 minutes, or until well puffed. Drain on paper. Sprinkle with confectioners' sugar. Serve.

Little Sausages and Apple Rings

Goes well with eggs and French toast. Plan on 3 sausages and about 3 apple rings per person.

**18 sausage links,
   cooked according to
   package directions**
4 medium-size apples
⅓ cup pineapple juice

Wash and core apples. Cut each crosswise into about 5 slices. Place apple slices flat in the skillet. Add pineapple juice. Cover and cook about 5 minutes over medium heat on one side. Turn apples and cook about 5 minutes, or until slices are tender. Remove from skillet and serve with sausage links.

Heavenly Pie

One of the great things about this pie is that you must make it at least the day before serving. This is very light and is a real favorite. Serves 6-8.

1½ cups sugar
**¼ teaspoon cream of
   tartar**
4 eggs, separated
**3 tablespoons lemon
   juice**
**1 tablespoon lemon
   rind, finely grated**
1 pint heavy cream

Sift together 1 cup sugar and cream of tartar. Beat egg whites until stiff, but not dry. Gradually add sugar mixture and continue beating until thoroughly blended. Use to line bottom and sides of a 9-inch, well-greased pie plate, hollowing out center and being careful not to spread too close to the rim. Bake at 275° for 1 hour. Cool.

Beat egg yolks slightly in top of double boiler, then stir in remaining ½ cup sugar, lemon rind and lemon juice. Cook 8-10 minutes.

Remove from heat and cool. Whip cream. Combine half of it with lemon-egg mixture and use to fill meringue shell. Cover with remaining whipped cream. Cover with plastic wrap and refrigerate approximately 24 hours.

SURPRISE BABY SHOWER BRUNCH
Serves 8

Fresh Fruit Float *

Swimming Shrimp *

Eggs Blackstone
(English Muffin, Fried Tomato, Crumbled
Bacon, Poached Egg, Hollandaise Sauce)

Tangerine-Walnut Toss *

Shortcut Cheese and Herb Biscuits *

Mocha Treat **

Coffee and Tea

Whether this is the first baby or the fourth, expectant mothers love showers and gifts. Brunch is a perfect occasion for getting the gals together to take time out from busy schedules to honor a good friend. She will be pleased and flattered that her shower is done around a spectacular brunch. The light and refreshing Fresh Fruit Float appetizer will freshen your guests' palates for the Swimming Shrimp and the fantastic Eggs Blackstone which follow. The Mocha Treat can be done ahead. It looks and tastes simply super, and the hostess will enjoy the fact that it comes directly from the freezer.

Table Setting

Check with your local department store and children's specialty shops. Very often they have baby shower decorations which they will either lend or rent at a very nominal fee. Your stationery store also sells a varied assortment of paper table decorations with matching napkins and cups. If you do not want to use this type of centerpiece, fresh flowers are always appropriate. A delicate white Madeira cloth will be the perfect table cover and white linen napkins will look lovely with your good china and silver. Your honored guest will always remember this surprise shower.

*Do ahead
**Freeze

Fresh Fruit Float

This can be your beverage and your fruit course. Use pretty glass dishes or parfait glasses. Very refreshing. Makes 1 serving.

**fruit, such as raspber-
ries, blueberries,
banana slices, sliced
strawberries
ginger ale
1 scoop lime sherbet**

Fill tall glass with fruit. Pour in chilled ginger ale. Top with lime sherbet.

Swimming Shrimp

Serve with toothpicks in a pretty dish. A lovely appetizer.

**1-1½ pounds medium
shrimp, cooked and
cleaned**

Sauce:
1½ cups mayonnaise
¾ cup catsup
**⅛ teaspoon Tabasco
sauce**
**2½ tablespoons lemon
juice**

Mix all the ingredients for the sauce and refrigerate. Add shrimp to sauce and put in a lovely bowl and serve.

Eggs Blackstone

A dear friend suggested this recipe many times; I finally got the message and must pass on this really great treat to you. One of these is fine per person if you are having lots of other things with it. If not, make two. As a matter of fact, you might make two per person anyway —they will not be wasted! Makes 8 servings.

**4 English muffins, split,
toasted and buttered**
8 ¾-inch slices tomato
**8 slices bacon, cooked
and crumbled**
8 poached eggs
**2 cups Hollandaise
Sauce (See page 90)**

Dip the tomato slices in flour and fry in bacon fat. Place a tomato slice on half an English muffin, then some crumbled bacon. Top with a poached egg, cover it with Hollandaise Sauce and a few more small pieces of bacon.

Tangerine-Walnut Toss

A very nice and refreshing salad. Makes 8 servings.

8 cups torn lettuce
2 cups tangerine sections, membrane removed
½ cup olive oil
⅓ cup vinegar
2 tablespoons water
1 medium onion, sliced
1 tablespoon sugar
1 clove garlic, minced
1 teaspoon celery seeds
½ teaspoon salt
dash of pepper

½ cup walnut pieces
1 tablespoon butter
¼ teaspoon salt

Place lettuce and tangerine sections in salad bowl; chill. Place olive oil, vinegar, water, onion, sugar, garlic, celery seeds, salt and pepper in a saucepan. Bring to a boil; remove from heat and chill. Just before serving, pour dressing over lettuce and tangerine sections; toss well. Sauté walnuts in butter and salt. Stir until walnuts are crisp and butter browned. Sprinkle over salad.

Shortcut Cheese and Herb Biscuits

A nice change. Makes 1½ dozen rolls.

1 loaf frozen bread dough
1 tablespoon butter, melted
¼ cup shredded Parmesan cheese
¼ teaspoon dill weed
¼ teaspoon salt
1 tablespoon butter, melted

1 tablespoon parsley flakes

Let bread dough thaw and rise as directed on package. Grease a 9-inch layer cake pan. Shape loaf into 18 balls. Dip balls into 1 tablespoon melted butter, then dip tops into cheese and arrange in pan. Mix dill weed, salt and 1 tablespoon melted butter. Brush dill mixture on rolls in pan; sprinkle with parsley flakes. Bake 15 minutes.

Mocha Treat

A delicious and easy dessert. Serves 8.

2 packages coconut macaroons, crushed
¼ cup rum (add as desired)
1 quart mocha ice cream
1 cup heavy cream
½ teaspoon instant coffee
semisweet chocolate shavings

Add rum to macaroons until it reaches a thick, dry, pasty consistency. Press macaroon mixture to sides of compote or individual sherbet dishes. Fill containers with mocha ice cream and round off top with back of spoon. Cover with aluminum foil and freeze. Whip cream, adding instant coffee while whipping. Top the dessert with whipped cream and shaved chocolate.

EASTER WEEKEND BRUNCH
Serves 10

1-2-3 Easy Punch
Fresh Pineapple Wedges *
Cheese Soufflé With Eggs
and Sauce Florentine *
Oven Tomatoes With Cornflakes *
Pecan Muffins **
Meringue-Cake Special *
Coffee

Invite your children and grandchildren for a Saturday Easter Egg Hunt and brunch. Before your guests arrive you can be preparing the menu and setting the table while your husband is hiding lots of colored eggs and small candies — outside, if the weather permits! No one is too old to get into the spirit so that even your grown-up children will be a part of the act. The menu is easy and varied and will be pleasing to all age groups. You will not have to spend much time in the kitchen, so you can enjoy the fun. The sparkling punch will be enjoyed by everyone and the young ones will love drinking the same thing as the parents.

Table Setting

A pastel tablecloth with matching napkins will not detract from the center of your table. For your focal point, fill a shallow breadbasket with Easter grass and attractively nest wooden, ceramic or stuffed bunnies and colored eggs. Fill tiny Easter baskets with colored grass and coated pastel mints and put one at each place with a different colored pastel bow on each handle as an added attraction. Flowered pottery dishes will be suitable and cheerful. Use the silverware that you feel goes best with your dishes. With all your special decorations and lovely foods, everyone will have a wonderful and memorable day.

*Do ahead
**Freeze

1-2-3 Easy Punch

Very easy and light. Makes 10 servings.

1 can (6 ounces) frozen
   orange juice concen-
   trate
⅓ cup light corn syrup
1 bottle (1 pint, 12
   ounces) ginger ale

orange slices
whole strawberries
ice cubes or block of ice

Combine all ingredients in a punch bowl.

Fresh Pineapple Wedges

This looks pretty and will not spoil appetites. Serves 12.

2 good-sized ripe
   pineapples
cherries or straw-
   berries

Cut each pineapple in half right through the crown, and cut each half into three wedges — each wedge will have leaves at the end. Remove the strip of core from each wedge with a knife. Cut pieces, but do not remove from shell. Stick tooth-picks in some of the pieces and add a cherry or strawberry at the end. Serve cold.

Cheese Soufflé with Eggs and Sauce Florentine

This is a three-layer casserole and it looks lovely in a glass soufflé dish. Serves 10-12.

3 packages (9 ounces
   each) frozen
   creamed spinach
8 hard-cooked eggs,
   peeled and halved
1 medium onion, chopped
6 tablespoons butter
6 tablespoons flour
½ teaspoon salt
1 teaspoon dry mustard
1½ cups milk
⅛ teaspoon bottled
   red-pepper season-
   ing
6 eggs, separated
1½ cups shredded
   Swiss or Muenster
   cheese

Heat spinach, following package directions; pour into greased 3-quart glass soufflé dish. Arrange cut surfaces of hard-cooked egg halves against side of dish. In a small saucepan sauté onion in butter until soft. Blend in flour, salt and mustard; cook, stirring constantly, just until bubbly. Stir in milk and red-pepper seasoning; continue cooking and stirring until sauce thickens and bubbles 1 minute. Remove from heat. Sauce will be thick. Beat egg yolks into sauce, one at a time, beating well after each addition. Beat egg whites just until they form soft peaks in a large bowl. Stir about ¼ of egg whites into sauce; stir in cheese; fold into remaining egg whites. Carefully pour on top of spinach. Bake at 350° for 45 minutes, or until puffed and golden brown. Serve at once.

Oven Tomatoes with Cornflakes

A colorful and tasty addition to the menu. Very easy to make. Serves 10.

10 medium tomatoes,
   cut in half
½ cup butter
2 teaspoons seasoned
   salt

1½ teaspoons garlic
   powder
1½ teaspoons dill weed
1½ cups cornflake
   crumbs

Combine all ingredients except the tomatoes. Spread the mixture over cut
side of tomatoes. Place in shallow dish
and refrigerate overnight. Bake at 300°
for 35 minutes.

Pecan Muffins

Serve warm with butter. Yield: 18 muffins.

2 cups sifted flour
4 teaspoons baking
   powder
½ teaspoon salt
½ cup sugar
1 cup milk
1 egg
¼ cup melted shorten-
   ing

½ cup chopped pecans

Sift dry ingredients. Combine milk and
well-beaten egg; blend in shortening.
Add with nuts to dry ingredients and
beat enough to mix well. Pour into well
greased muffin pans, filling ⅔ full. Bake
at 350° for 35 minutes. Wrap securely
with aluminum foil to freeze and then
reheat.

Meringue-Cake Special

*This has got to be one of the most delicious and spectacular desserts
ever. Any fruit can be used with the whipped cream for the filling. Serves
10.*

½ package white cake
   mix (about 2 cups)
4 egg whites
⅛ teaspoon salt
1 cup sugar, sifted
1 teaspoon vanilla
½ cup shredded al-
   monds

Filling:

1 cup heavy cream
1 teaspoon vanilla
1½ cups sliced straw-
   berries and blueber-
   ries, sweetened

Mix ½ package white cake mix as directed on package. Pour into two
greased and floured 9-inch layer cake
pans. Beat 4 egg whites with salt until
stiff. Add the sugar very slowly (½ teaspoonful at a time). Beat constantly.
When all the sugar has been added, continue to beat for several minutes. Fold in
1 teaspoon vanilla. Spread the meringue
lightly over the cake batter in both pans.
Stud one meringue with the blanched
and shredded almonds, placing the
shreds very close together. Bake at 325°
for 40 minutes. Permit the cakes to cool
in the pans.

Filling: Whip cream until stiff, fold in
vanilla. Add sweetened fruit to whipped
cream.

Shortly before serving the cake, place
one layer, meringue-side-down, on a
cake platter. Spread the filling over it.
Place the almond-studded layer,
meringue-side-up, on the fruit-cream
filling. Refrigerate until ready to serve.

MAY

FAREWELL BRUNCH
Serves 4

Rum Fizz

Chilled Honeydew Melon/Lime Sherbet

Fried Eggs — Over Easy

Filets Mignons

Cold Tomatoes Filled with Mushrooms
and Artichokes *

Apricot Nut Bread **

Coffee

This is the time of year when many people are getting ready to move. Soon school will be closed and it will be time to pack up and leave for the new city that will be home for a while. Since your friends' schedule will be busy, brunch is a really good way to have a farewell get-together. With just four of you for brunch, you can cook and serve in the kitchen. You will be with your guests while they sip their rum fizzes at your kitchen table and you will not miss a bit of the conversation. Because this is a small group, the menu features some foods that cannot be prepared ahead.

Table Setting

Because you will be serving and eating in the kitchen, all you will need are brightly colored placemats and napkins with your everyday china and stainless flatware. A farewell gift wrapped in colors to complement your kitchen decor will make an unusual centerpiece. When unwrapped, this token of your friendship is on display in the center of your table for the rest of your meal.

*Do ahead
**Freeze

Rum Fizz

Easy and good. Makes 1 drink.

cracked ice
1 jigger light rum
1 jigger orange juice
ginger ale
orange slices for gar-
nish

Fill short glass ¾ full with cracked ice. Add rum and orange juice. Fill to top with ginger ale and garnish with an orange slice.

Chilled Honeydew Melon/Lime Sherbet

Very refreshing and light. Serves 4.

1 honeydew melon
1 pint lime sherbet

Fill ¼ of a (seeded) honeydew melon with lime sherbet and serve.

Fried Eggs — Over Easy

Excellent with steak. Serves 4.

4 fresh eggs
butter

Melt butter in frying pan over moderate heat. Add eggs as soon as the butter starts to sizzle. When white of egg is set, turn the egg over carefully. Remove from pan in about 15 seconds.

Filets Mignons

This is for a special treat. Really delicious. Serves 4.

½ cup soy sauce
⅓ cup salad oil
1 garlic clove, minced
½ teaspoon ginger
4 beef tenderloin
   steaks, each cut
   about 1 inch thick
4 slices French bread,
   each cut diagonally
   about 1½ inches
   thick
butter

Combine soy sauce, salad oil, garlic and ginger in a shallow dish. Add steaks and turn over to coat with marinade; arrange steaks in one layer. Cover and refrigerate for a few hours, turning meat occasionally. Preheat broiler. Place bread slices on cookie sheet; spread with butter. Broil bread 2 or 3 minutes until golden. Keep warm. Place steaks on greased rack in broiling pan; broil about 10 minutes for rare, turning once. Serve steaks on bread with pan drippings.

Cold Tomatoes Filled with Mushrooms and Artichokes

These tomatoes taste as good as they look. Aside from being a little different, they can be made the day before and there is no cooking involved – that is, except for the boiling water.

4 large firm tomatoes
seasoned salt (Lawry's is good)
seasoned pepper (Lawry's)
1 jar (6 ounces) marinated artichoke hearts, drained
3 cans (3½ ounces each) mushroom stems and pieces, drained
½ cup mayonnaise
⅓ cup sour cream
1 teaspoon curry powder

1 teaspoon lemon juice
1 tablespoon instant minced onion
paprika

Dip tomatoes in boiling water for 10 seconds, then run under cold water. Peel and scoop out pulp and seeds to form a cup. Sprinkle generously with seasoned salt and pepper; fill with artichokes and mushrooms. Refrigerate. In a bowl, combine mayonnaise, sour cream, curry, lemon juice and onion. Refrigerate. When ready to serve, top each tomato with the mayonnaise mixture and sprinkle with paprika.

Apricot Nut Bread

This can be made ahead of time and frozen. You may wish to serve this warm, although it is delicious cold. Easy to prepare. Makes 1 loaf.

½ cup dried apricots, diced
1 cup water
1 egg, well-beaten
1 cup sugar
2 tablespoons butter, melted
2 cups flour, sifted
1 tablespoon baking powder
¼ teaspoon baking soda
¾ teaspoon salt
½ cup orange juice
¼ cup water
1 cup almonds, sliced

Preheat oven to 350°. Soak apricots in 1 cup water for 30 minutes. Grease loaf pan. Beat egg until light; add sugar and blend well. Add butter. Sift flour with baking powder, soda and salt. Add alternately with orange juice and water. Add nuts and apricots which have been drained and diced and blend well. Bake 1½ hours.

SWEET SIXTEEN BRUNCH
Serves 10

Tea Base Punch *
Swiss Cheese Pie *
Five-Cup Salad *
Corn Sticks *
Chocolate Mousse *

When your daughter becomes 16, you will want to entertain her and her friends in a special way. A brunch is different and very grown-up. The Tea Base Punch can be served while your daughter is opening her gifts. This all-do-ahead menu features new taste combinations for girls of this age and is filling at the same time. The Chocolate Mousse, which substitutes for a birthday cake, is deliciously rich but light in texture and makes a great finale.

Table Setting

A pale blue linen tablecloth will highlight your lovely flowers. A soup tureen of sweet-smelling purple lilacs will dominate your table with their beauty and aroma. Individual nosegays of purple violets wrapped in doilies and tied with pale blue and white satin streamers can be placed at each girl's plate. Either light blue or white napkins will go well on your table. Since the service plate will only hold 3 items, dessert plates or special luncheon plates can be used. This is a table setting, a meal and an occasion that your daughter will never forget.

*Do ahead
**Freeze

Tea Base Punch

It is always good to have a nice recipe for a simple punch. Makes almost 3 quarts.

⅔ cup strong hot tea
1¾ cups sugar
1½ cups orange juice
1 cup lemon juice
1 quart chilled ginger ale
1 quart club soda
orange slices

Add sugar to hot tea and stir until sugar is dissolved. Add the orange and lemon juices and chill this syrup. Place large pieces of ice in a bowl or pitcher. Pour the syrup over it. Add ginger ale and club soda and serve. Use orange slices for garnish in glasses.

Swiss Cheese Pie

The very nice owner of an excellent little shop in Millburn, New Jersey, the Golden Pineapple, was nice enough to donate this delicious recipe. The crust is the best ever. Makes 2 pies — each serves 6 generously.

Foolproof Piecrust:

4 cups all-purpose flour

1¾ cups Crisco shortening

1 tablespoon sugar

2 teaspoons salt

1 tablespoon vinegar

1 egg

½ cup water

Filling:

1 pound Swiss cheese, grated

2 tablespoons flour

6 eggs, well beaten

2 cups milk

salt

pepper

(ground-up ham goes very well in this — optional)

Piecrust: With a fork, mix together flour, shortening, sugar and salt. In a separate bowl beat salt, vinegar, egg and water. Combine the two mixtures, stirring with a fork until all ingredients are moistened. Mold dough into a ball with hands. Chill at least 15 minutes before rolling into desired shape.

NOTE: 1. May be left in refrigerator up to 3 days.
2. May be frozen until ready to use.
3. Will remain soft in the refrigerator and can be taken out and rolled at once.
4. Enough for two 9-inch double crust pies and one 9-inch shell.

Filling: Dredge cheese with flour and arrange evenly in two 9-inch pie plates with unbaked pie shells. Combine eggs with milk, season lightly with salt and pepper and pour mixture over grated cheese (and ham). Bake at 400° for 15 minutes. Reduce heat to 325° and bake 30 minutes or until inserted knife comes out clean.

Five-Cup Salad

Really delicious and easy. Serves 10.

1 cup mandarin oranges

1 cup crushed pineapple

1 cup miniature marshmallows

1 cup shredded coconut

1 cup sour cream

Combine all ingredients and mix well. Serve on a bed of lettuce. Better if made the day before.

Corn Sticks

These go well with any meal. Yield: 14 sticks.

2 cups cornmeal
1½ teaspoons salt
2 cups buttermilk
2 eggs
1 teaspoon soda
1 teaspoon baking
  powder
4 tablespoons bacon
  grease

Preheat oven to 450°. Grease corn-stick pan with bacon grease, place in oven to preheat. Add salt to cornmeal, then buttermilk and eggs. Beat well; stir in soda and baking powder. Add hot grease from corn-stick pan, mixing well. Fill sections of hot pan ⅔ full. Bake 15 minutes or until brown.

Chocolate Mousse

An elegant finish to any meal. This can be put into a variety of containers: ring mold with whipped cream in the center garnished with shaved semisweet chocolate, parfait glasses, soufflé dish or individual dessert cups. Serves 12.

1 package (12 ounces)
  semisweet chocolate
  morsels
12 eggs, separated
2 teaspoons vanilla
  extract or 2 table-
  spoons any fruit-
  flavored brandy
3 teaspoons instant cof-
  fee powder
4 tablespoons confec-
  tioners' sugar, sifted
2 cups heavy cream
2 squares (1 ounce
  each) semisweet
  chocolate for garnish

Melt chocolate pieces in double boiler and remove from heat. With rubber spatula, rapidly stir in egg yolks all at once; stir in vanilla. Beat egg whites until stiff peaks form; with rubber spatula, gently fold beaten whites into chocolate mixture. Spoon mixture into dessert dishes. Refrigerate at least a few hours. Place coffee powder and sugar in a bowl; add cream. With mixer at medium speed, beat just until soft peaks form. To serve, top mousse with whipped cream mixture and grated chocolate for garnish.

DERBY DAY BRUNCH
Serves 16

Mint Juleps
Cheese Fondue *
Easy Chicken Crepes *
French-Style Green Beans
Bing Cherry Salad Mold *
Zucchini Bread **
Whiskey Cake **
Coffee

Derby Day brunches are becoming more and more popular. This menu has to be the best ever for Derby Day. The Mint Juleps create a Southern atmosphere and are complemented by the hearty Cheese Fondue which sets the tone for a really superb menu. The Easy Chicken Crepes are simple to prepare for a crowd, as are the green beans and the do-ahead Bing Cherry Salad Mold. The Whiskey Cake has to be tasted to be believed — you will find the men asking you to give the recipe to their wives. However you set it up, make sure that every guest has placed a bet, as this makes the Kentucky Derby more exciting.

Table Setting
Since the Kentucky Derby is popularly known as "The Run for the Roses," it is a good idea to use roses in your centerpiece. Arrange a low bowl of red roses on a white tablecloth and lay a horseshoe on each side of the bowl. Ivy can be entwined around the bowl and the horseshoes. To further carry out the racing theme, use bright-colored thin satin ribbons to tie around your silverware rolled up in white napkins. Plain china will probably look best with your colorful buffet table.

*Do ahead
**Freeze

Mint Juleps

These potent drinks are traditionally popular on Derby Day! Makes 1 serving.

4 sprigs mint
1 teaspoon sugar
finely crushed ice
1½ jiggers bourbon

In a chilled highball glass or tankard (preferably silver or aluminum), place 3 sprigs mint and sugar. Crush mint with handle of wooden spoon until sugar is dissolved, about 5 minutes. Fill glass to brim with ice; pour in bourbon. Add more ice to fill glass, without stirring. Set in freezer until serving time. Just before serving, garnish with a sprig of mint dusted with powdered sugar.

Cheese Fondue

This is a really "fun" appetizer to serve. It tastes delicious. Just make sure you set the casserole or fondue pot on a tray. Serves 16 as an appetizer.

1 clove garlic
3 cups Neuchatel or
   dry white wine
2 pounds natural
   Gruyère cheese,
   grated
4 teaspoons cornstarch
6 tablespoons kirsch or
   sherry
freshly ground black
   pepper

Rub the bottom and sides of an earthenware casserole or fondue pot with the garlic. Add the wine and heat to the boiling point, but do not boil. Add the cheese, stirring constantly with a wooden spoon. When the cheese is creamy and barely simmering, add the cornstarch blended with the kirsch. Stir until the mixture bubbles. Add pepper to taste. Place the casserole over an alcohol burner with a low flame. Keep the fondue hot but not simmering. If it becomes too thick, add a little more wine. To serve, accompany with cubes of crusty bread for dipping into the casserole of melted cheese.

Easy Chicken Crepes

You can make the crepes ahead and freeze. Fill before your guests arrive and refrigerate until ready to heat. These are very tasty and do not take much time. Use a few crepe pans, otherwise you will be forever making enough to serve a crowd. Makes approximately 32-34 crepes. Serves 16-18.

3 cups sifted flour
½ teaspoon salt
3 cups milk
6 tablespoons melted
   butter
6 eggs, beaten

Filling:

3 cans (10½ ounces each) condensed cream of chicken soup, undiluted

3 cans (3 ounces each) chopped mushrooms, drained

6 cups cooked chicken, cut in small pieces

3 pints sour cream

Cheddar cheese, grated

Crepes: Add milk and butter to eggs. Stir into flour and salt. Beat until smooth. Grease skillet or crepe pan and heat. Pour in approximately 2½-3 tablespoons batter. Tilt pan quickly until batter covers about 5-inch area. Turn when pancake is brown on bottom and brown other side. Use foil, waxed paper or paper towels between crepes and leave at room temperature (wrapped) if you prepare a day ahead.

Filling: Combine first three ingredients in saucepan, using some of the liquid from the mushrooms. Stir and heat thoroughly. Add sour cream.

Fill crepes with chicken mixture and roll and place seam-side-down in greased shallow baking dish. Garnish with grated cheese and bake at 375° for 20 minutes or until just bubbly — do not overcook.

French-Style Green Beans

Use 3 large bags of frozen green beans. Butter and salt and pepper. Slightly undercook. Looks nice on a plate and goes well with the crepes and salad.

Bing Cherry Salad Mold

This is a great molded salad. Serves 16-18.

3 cans (1 pound each) Bing cherries

3 packages (3 ounces each) black-cherry gelatin

2¼ cups hot water

1½ cups dry sherry

2¼ cups cherry syrup

1½ cups sour cream

1½ cups thin sliced almonds, crumbled

Drain cherries, saving 2¼ cups syrup. Dissolve gelatin in hot water. Add sherry and cherry syrup. Chill until slightly thickened. Add cherries, sour cream and almonds. Pour into a large mold and chill. Unmold on a bed of lettuce.

Zucchini Bread

My mother-in-law is always sending us a loaf of this bread and we all love it. This freezes well. Makes 2 loaves.

3 eggs
1 cup brown sugar
1 cup white sugar
1 cup vegetable oil
1 tablespoon vanilla
2 cups sifted flour
1 tablespoon cinnamon
2 teaspoons baking
    soda
1 teaspoon salt
¼ teaspoon baking
    powder
2 cups coarsely grated
    zucchini, loosely
    packed
1 cup chopped nuts

In a bowl beat eggs until fluffy. Beat in sugar, oil and vanilla until it is thick and lemon colored. Add rest of ingredients and pour into 2 loaf pans and bake at 350° for 50-60 minutes. Invert on racks and let cool completely.

Whiskey Cake

A few years back, a very good friend from Farmington, Connecticut, brought this when she and her family came to visit for the weekend. We all devoured it in no time, and since then, I have used it on many occasions. Easy to make and looks nice when you do it in a bundt cake pan. Makes 1 cake.

1 package yellow cake
    mix
1 small package instant
    vanilla pudding
4 eggs
1 cup milk
1½ ounces rye (1 jig-
    ger)
½ cup vegetable oil
1 cup chopped walnuts
    or pecans, floured

Glaze:

1 stick butter (8 table-
    spoons)
¾ cup sugar
½ cup rye

Combine first 7 ingredients and mix well. Grease and flour bundt pan. Bake at 350° for 1 hour, or until toothpick comes out clean.

Glaze: Melt 3 ingredients together. Pour ⅔ of glaze on top of cake while cake is right out of oven and still in pan. Leave cake in pan 25 minutes. Remove from pan, pour over remaining glaze.

JUNE

FATHER'S DAY BRUNCH
Serves 6

Bloody Marys
Eggs Benedict
Fresh Asparagus
Strawberry Dream Angel Cake *
Coffee or Tea

Father's Day is a must for a family get-together. Daytime entertaining is sensible when you are together with your children as well as your parents, and brunch is a special way to say "Happy Father's Day" to your husband and your father. The family can gather in the late morning to present dad and grandfather with gifts and then enjoy a hearty brunch. Men like simple food; this special menu planned for them will please the children as well as the adults. Since you are comfortable entertaining your parents, some last minute cooking can be a family affair and everyone will appreciate the touch of elegance this meal provides. After the sumptuous brunch, a game of badminton would be an enjoyable way to end the Father's Day party.

Table Setting
To honor the fathers in the family, a bright linen cloth with your silver and china will be lovely on your dining room table for a sit-down brunch. A centerpiece with a masculine flavor can be made using a man's straw skimmer hat piled high with peaches, plums and clusters of grapes.

*Do ahead

Bloody Mary
My husband is great at making a Bloody Mary, and this has become a popular request at our house. We always keep large cans of Clamato juice on hand, and our children enjoy having their own cocktails with all the trimmings and no vodka. Makes 1 serving.

Clamato Juice
1 jigger vodka
¼ wedge lime or lemon
dash of celery salt
dash of Tabasco or hot
    pepper sauce
    (optional)

dash of Worcestershire
    sauce (optional)

Pour 1 jigger vodka into each tall glass. Squeeze and drop in a wedge of lime or lemon and seasonings. Fill glass with ice cubes and fill to top with Clamato juice. Stir and serve.

Eggs Benedict

(Poached eggs on slices of ham and toasted English muffins topped with Hollandaise Sauce)

The rich-and-famous one-and-only you always order at a special restaurant. This is a real treat for your brunch. Serves 6.

Hollandaise Sauce

9 egg yolks

6 tablespoons lemon
   juice

½ teaspoon salt

3 cups butter, melted

Place yolks, lemon juice and salt in blender container; cover and turn to high speed for 4 seconds. Remove cover and add the melted butter in a thin, steady stream. Sauce will be done in 30 seconds. Place blender in pan of warm water until ready to serve.

Eggs Benedict

6 English muffins, split

butter

12 slices ham, sautéed

12 poached eggs

Hollandaise Sauce

Toast and butter English muffins and place 2 halves on each serving plate. Top each with a slice of ham, then a poached egg. Spoon Hollandaise Sauce over each egg. Garnish with watercress.

Fresh Asparagus

Peeling makes the difference. Delicious with any meal, this springtime delicacy blends perfectly with the flavor of the Hollandaise Sauce on the Eggs Benedict. Serves 6.

24 spears fresh as-
   paragus

Wash all the asparagus at one time in cold water. With a sharp knife or vegetable peeler, peel off outer skin on the lower half of each spear. Cut off darkened butt end. Place asparagus in cold water until ready to cook. To cook, place asparagus in boiling salted water, cover and cook 9-12 minutes at low boil.

Strawberry Dream Angel Cake

This really looks so good you'll want to eat the whole thing yourself. It is a good recipe to use up the egg whites from the Hollandaise Sauce. However, you may wish to use an angel food cake package mix; it's easier, and you can make Chocolate Macaroon Cookies with some of those leftover egg whites. This cake tastes better if you refrigerate it overnight. The recipe easily feeds 10-12; however, you will want some left-over.

Angel Food Cake

1 cup pre-sifted flour
¾ cup plus 2 table-
  spoons sugar
1½ cups egg whites
  (12)
1½ teaspoons cream of
  tartar
¼ teaspoon salt
¾ cup sugar
1½ teaspoons vanilla
½ teaspoon almond
  flavoring

Heat oven to 375°. Have ready a tube pan, 10×4 inches (ungreased). Stir flour and first amount of sugar together to blend. Measure egg whites, cream of tartar and salt into large mixing bowl. Beat until foamy. Gradually add second amount of sugar, 2 tablespoons at a time. Continue beating until meringue holds stiff peaks. Fold in flavorings. Sprinkle flour-sugar mixture over meringue. Fold in gently just until the flour-sugar mixture disappears. Push batter into tube pan. Gently cut through batter to prevent large holes. Bake 30-35 minutes (until no imprint remains when finger lightly touches top of cake). Invert on a funnel or soda bottle. Let hang until cool. Remove from pan.

Frosting

1 pint strawberries,
  sliced (2 cups)
½ cup confectioners'
  sugar, sifted
1 pint heavy cream (2
  cups)

Chill medium-size metal bowl and beaters. Whip cream until stiff peaks form, adding sugar gradually. Fold in strawberries and refrigerate. Cut angel cake crosswise into 3 layers. Spread a little frosting over first layer. Repeat for second layer. Top with third cake layer. Frost side and top of cake with remaining strawberry cream mixture. Refrigerate.

WEDDING PARTY BRUNCH
Serves 12

Sparkling Strawberry Wine Punch
with
Fancy Fruit Ice Ring *
Svenska Ägg ock Räkor med Dillsås *
(Swedish Eggs and Shrimp
with Dill Sauce)
Rice
Spinach Salad *
Bread Sticks *
(Bakery)
Delicious Filbert Slices **
Coffee and Tea

Brunch is a terrific way to entertain members of wedding parties and out-of-town guests. If a friend or relative is involved in a wedding, she will appreciate your inviting people to have brunch together. The time of day is perfect. On the day of an afternoon wedding, people will have a chance to meet some of the bride's and groom's family, or on the day following the ceremony, new friends will enjoy reminiscing about the wedding and reception. Be ready for the oohs and aahs: the Fancy Fruit Ice Ring is certain to bring many compliments.

Table Setting

A light and lovely setting can be created by using a yellow sheet or paper liner under a white lace or organdy tablecloth. A lace-bordered yellow and white nosegay tied with narrow yellow satin ribbons ending in love knots arranged with a pair of crystal or silver birds makes an appropriate centerpiece. White china, silver, crystal and yellow linen napkins tied with white satin bows complete your elegant table setting. This is the time to get out your grandmother's cut-glass punch bowl!

 *Do ahead
**Freeze

Sparkling Strawberry Wine Punch with Fancy Fruit Ice Ring

This will not knock your guests over – count on 3 or 4 punch glasses per person. Wait until you get the phone calls requesting this recipe! Makes about 40 servings.

Ice Ring:

2 oranges

2 lemons

Punch:

1 can (6 ounces) frozen lemonade concentrate

6 cups (1 large can) pineapple juice

2 bottles white table wine

1 large bottle club soda

1 pint strawberries, washed

Prepare the day before, at least. Cut thin slices of oranges and lemons in half. In the bottom of a ring mold that will fit the top of your punch bowl or tureen, arrange fruit slices alternately, overlapping slightly. Add just enough water to cover slices. Freeze. Then fill mold with water and freeze.

Combine frozen lemonade and pineapple juice in a punch bowl or tureen. Add wine and club soda. Mix well. Unmold Ice Ring and add to punch. Float whole strawberries in punch for garnish.

Svenska Ägg ock Räkor med Dillsås (Swedish Eggs with Shrimp and Dill Sauce)

These delicate and different-tasting eggs are spectacular. My Swedish friend gave me the basis for this recipe. Try to use fresh dill and lots of it (2 bunches!) Serves 12.

16 hard-cooked eggs

1½ pounds shrimp, cooked and cleaned (add 1 bunch dill to cooking water)

¼ cup butter

1 bunch scallions, sliced thin, including 1 inch of green tops

5 tablespoons flour

2½ cups chicken broth (use 3 bouillon cubes and boiling water)

½ cup clam juice

½ cup dry white wine

1 cup heavy cream

4 tablespoons chopped fresh dill or 2 tablespoons dry dill weed

1½ cups shredded Parmesan cheese

Melt butter in heavy saucepan, add onions and ½ cup cold water. Bring to boil, then reduce heat to moderate and cook until all water has boiled away. Stir in flour and cook 3 minutes — do not brown. Add broth, wine, clam juice, cream and dill. Cook, whipping constantly with wire whisk until sauce comes to a boil. Stir in ½ of cheese. Take off heat. Set aside. Halve hard-cooked eggs lengthwise and place yolk-side-up in a flat 3-quart pyrex baking dish.

Cover with layer of shrimp. Pour sauce on top of eggs and shrimp. Top with remaining cheese. Garnish with more dill. Refrigerate. Let stand at room temperature about 30 minutes. Bake uncovered at 400° for 20 minutes, til hot and bubbly. Serve with rice.

Rice

Follow directions on your favorite package.

Spinach Salad

Easily made for any size crowd – looks really green. Everything can be done ahead. Just toss at the last minute. Serves 12.

2½ pounds fresh
   spinach
½ pound sliced fresh
   mushrooms
8 strips bacon, crisply
   cooked and crumbled
1 large Bermuda onion,
   sliced thin

2 cups Good Seasons or
   other mild Italian
   dressing, mixed as
   directed on package

Use spinach leaves only. Wash carefully and thoroughly and tear into pieces. Toss all ingredients and serve.

Delicious Filbert Slices

These are really easy, fun to do, and they freeze well. Makes 30.

1¼ pounds filbert nuts,
   pulverized in
   blender
1 cup sugar
1 tablespoon grated
   lemon rind
2 eggs
confectioners' sugar

Preheat oven to 350°. In bowl, mix first three ingredients thoroughly. Make a well in center, drop in eggs and mix well with hands until dough holds together. Divide batter in half and roll each half on waxed paper in roll approximately 20 inches long, flouring hands if necessary as you roll dough. Flatten rolls in oblongs about 2 inches wide and cut in diagonal 1½-inch slices. Dust very lightly with flour and place about 1 inch apart on ungreased baking sheets. Bake approximately 15 minutes. Roll in confectioners' sugar and store in an airtight container.

GRADUATION BRUNCH
Serves 16

Sunshine Punch *
Sausage and Cheese Surprise *
Frozen Cranberry Salad **
Sour Cream Coffee Cake **
Crunchy Chip Cookies *

Graduation is a great occasion for a brunch. Just think how delighted your daughter will be to have a memorable boy-girl daytime celebration the day after graduation. There will be yearbooks to sign and plans for the summer to be discussed. Since there is a great possibility you will be involved with graduation plans, this entire menu can be done ahead and some of the recipes can be frozen. A few decorations and paper dishes make this a very easy way to entertain.

Table Setting

A patio or pool is the perfect setting for a young people's brunch. The atmosphere is casual and it is a perfect occasion for decorative paper products. Some of the larger manufacturers of party products make paper and plastic items with a graduation motif. A picnic table for serving is used with or without a tablecloth. Potted geraniums tied with gingham bows surround a pretty basket. The graduate could help make mock diplomas with a poem or saying on them for each guest. These are closed with a gold seal and heaped in the basket.

*Do ahead
**Freeze

Sunshine Punch

Delicious for any occasion. Prepare ahead. Makes 16 servings.

1 can (6 ounces) frozen orange juice concentrate

1 can (6 ounces) frozen lemonade concentrate

1 can (6 ounces) frozen limeade concentrate

5 cups cold water
1 quart 7-Up, chilled

Combine all ingredients except the 7-Up. Mix well. Chill. When ready to serve add the 7-Up.

Sausage and Cheese Surprise

This is a real favorite and a very special recipe. It is very easy to prepare and must be prepared the day before. You can easily use more or less of the sausage and cheese depending on what you have on hand (for an emergency dish!). Serves 6-8 (double it for 16).

8 slices firm white bread, decrusted and cubed

2 cups sharp Cheddar cheese, grated

2 pounds link sausage

5 eggs

2½ cups whole milk

¾ teaspoon dry mustard

1 can undiluted cream of mushroom soup

½ cup whole milk

Place bread in a greased 8×12-inch pan. Top with grated cheese. Brown sausage, cut into thirds and place on top of cheese. Beat eggs with 2½ cups milk and dry mustard. Pour over sausage, cover and refrigerate overnight. Before cooking, mix one can undiluted cream of mushroom soup with ½ cup whole milk. Bake at 300° for 1½ hours.

Frozen Cranberry Salad

This is a good dish to serve with any meal. Instead of using loaf pans, try using two 1-quart paper milk cartons. Cartons may be torn away and salad sliced in squares. Serves 16.

4 packages (3 ounces each) cream cheese, softened

4 tablespoons sugar

4 tablespoons mayonnaise

2 cans (1 pound each) jellied cranberry sauce

2 cups crushed pineapple, drained

1 cup chopped pecans

1 cup heavy cream, whipped

Cream together cheese and sugar; stir in mayonnaise. Fold in cranberry sauce, pineapple, nuts and whipped cream. Turn into two 9×5×3-inch loaf pans. Freeze until firm. Cut into slices. Serve on shredded lettuce.

Sour Cream Coffee Cake

This cake stays moist for days because of the sour cream. It also freezes well. The recipe makes one cake which will serve 12. Double this to take care of second helpings for most guests.

1 cup butter

2 cups sugar

2 eggs

1 cup sour cream

½ teaspoon vanilla

2 cups flour

1 teaspoon baking
powder

¼ teaspoon salt

Topping:

1½ tablespoons sugar

1 cup pecans, chopped

1 teaspoon cinnamon

Preheat oven to 350°. Cream butter. Add sugar gradually, beating until very light and fluffy. Beat in eggs, one at a time. Fold in sour cream and vanilla. Add flour sifted with baking powder and salt. Combine topping ingredients separately. Pour about one-third of the batter into a well-greased, floured bundt pan or a 9-inch tube pan. Sprinkle with three-fourths of topping mixture. Spoon in remaining batter. Sprinkle with remaining topping mixture. Bake 1 hour.

Crunchy Chip Cookies

These are somewhat like chocolate chip cookies. The Rice Krispies and raisins make them very tasty and different. The young people love to have these around – which isn't for long. Makes about 3½ dozen cookies.

1¼ cups flour

½ teaspoon baking
soda

¼ teaspoon salt

½ cup butter, softened

1 cup sugar

1 egg

1 teaspoon vanilla

2 cups Rice Krispies

1 cup semisweet choco-
late morsels

1 cup raisins

Preheat oven to 350°. In a small bowl, combine flour, soda and salt. Set aside. In a large bowl, combine butter and sugar and beat until creamy. Add egg and vanilla and mix well. Blend in flour mixture. Stir in Rice Krispies, chocolate morsels and raisins. Drop by level tablespoonfuls onto lightly greased cookie sheets. Bake 12-15 minutes.

JULY

COOLING MID-SUMMER BRUNCH

Serves 4

Gin and Tonic

Chilled Watercress Soup *

Cold Poached Salmon Steaks With Dill Sauce *

Frozen Avocado Molds **

Melba Toast With Sweet Butter *

Lemon Snow With Custard Sauce *

Coconut Kisses *

Iced Tea With Mint *

When the temperature soars, the last thing anyone wants to eat is hot food, and the last thing the hostess wants to prepare is hot food in her kitchen. This brunch menu is composed exclusively of cold foods which are tempting and delicious. Your guests will marvel at your mouth-watering Cold Poached Salmon Steaks With Dill Sauce. The Frozen Avocado Molds can be unmolded early in the day and then put back in the freezer ready to serve. As you will notice, all items can be prepared ahead so that you can work at your own pace and serve your brunch straight from the refrigerator. Cold soups look interesting in cookbooks, but too many people pass them by. Try one here — your guests will love it.

Table Setting

Keep plans for your table setting simple. If it is a lovely not-too-hot morning, eat on your patio or porch; or if it will be too hot for that, eat in an air-conditioned room in your house. Use pale-colored placemats, bright flowered napkins and for your centerpiece, use fresh cut flowers placed in a pretty pitcher. This is a perfect occasion to use glass plates.

*Do ahead
**Freeze

Gin and Tonic

A familiar and refreshing beverage. Makes 1 serving.

1 jigger gin
quinine water (tonic
    water)
lime or lemon slice or
    wedge
ice cubes

Over ice cubes in highball glass, pour gin; add quinine water to fill glass; add lime slice.

Chilled Watercress Soup

This an easy and delicious soup, hot or cold. Serves 4-6.

2 cans condensed
    cream of asparagus
    soup
½ cup cut-up
    watercress
2 soup-cans milk
¼ teaspoon basil

Blend undiluted soup and watercress in blender at low speed. In saucepan over medium heat, heat mixture with milk and basil. Do not let boil. Refrigerate. Serve hot or cold.

Cold Poached Salmon Steaks With Dill Sauce

A real delicacy, but easy to prepare. Serves 4.

4 salmon steaks, 1-inch
    thick (about 2½
    pounds)
3 chicken-bouillon
    cubes
2 tablespoons white
    vinegar
1 medium onion, sliced
1 bay leaf
dill weed
salt and pepper

Dill Sauce:

1 cup mayonnaise
2 tablespoons dill weed

In 12-inch skillet, combine 4 cups boiling water, bouillon cubes, vinegar, onion, bay leaf, 1 teaspoon salt, dash pepper and 1 teaspoon dill weed. Bring to a boil, then reduce to low; cover skillet and simmer 5 minutes. Add salmon steaks; cover and simmer 8 minutes. Remove with slotted spoon and cool. Wrap securely and refrigerate.

Dill Sauce: In small bowl, stir mayonnaise with dill weed with a fork, until well mixed. Refrigerate.

Serve cold salmon steaks with ¼ cup of sauce on each one. Garnish with dill weed.

Frozen Avocado Molds

Very unusual but quite tasty and easy to make. Serves 4-6.

4 tablespoons lemon
   juice
⅔ cup orange mar-
   malade
1 cup mashed avocado
1 cup whipped cream
1 cup blueberries

Combine lemon juice, orange mar-malade and avocado; fold in whipped cream. Spoon into 4-6 small molds. Freeze. Serve surrounded by blueber-ries on lettuce.

Melba Toast With Sweet Butter

Buy some good melba toast and spread with sweet butter.

Lemon Snow With Custard Sauce

This has to be an all-time favorite. Is there anything more refreshing? Serves 4-6.

Lemon Snow:

¾ cup sugar
1 envelope unflavored
   gelatin (1 table-
   spoon)
1¼ cups water
¼ cup fresh squeezed
   lemon juice
1 tablespoon grated
   lemon rind
2 egg whites

Snow: Mix sugar, gelatin and water in saucepan. Cook just until boiling, stir-ring constantly. Blend in lemon juice and rind. Place pan in refrigerator until mixture mounds when dropped from spoon. Beat egg whites until stiff. Slowly blend gelatin into beaten egg whites, using rotary beater. When blended, stir mixture with rubber spatula until it holds its shape. Spoon into a pretty glass or white soufflé dish. Chill until firm. Serve with Custard Sauce.

Custard Sauce:

1½ cups milk
4 egg yolks (or 2 whole
   eggs)
¼ cup sugar
¼ teaspoon salt
1 teaspoon vanilla

Custard Sauce: Scald milk in top of double boiler over direct heat. Beat egg yolks in small bowl. Blend in sugar and salt. Gradually stir in scalded milk. Re-turn to double boiler. Cook over sim-mering water, stirring constantly. When custard coats silver spoon (thin coat-ing), remove from heat. Cool quickly. Blend in vanilla.

Coconut Kisses

These are light and chewy. Makes 1½ dozen cookies.

2 egg whites
¾ cup sugar
⅛ teaspoon salt
¼ teaspoon vanilla
1¼ cups shredded
  coconut

Heat oven to 325°. Beat egg whites until frothy. Gradually beat in sugar. Continue beating until very stiff and glossy. Stir in salt, vanilla and coconut. Drop heaping teaspoonfuls 2 inches apart onto ungreased brown wrapping paper on baking sheet. Bake 20 minutes. Lift off paper, lay wet towel on hot baking sheet. Place paper of kisses on towel, let stand 1 minute. Steam will loosen kisses. Slip off with spatula.

Iced Tea With Mint

This always brings compliments. Makes 1½ quarts.

water
6 tea bags
2 stalks (4 inches each)
  fresh mint
¾ cup sugar
2 lemons, juice of

Boil 2 cups of water and remove from heat. Add tea bags and steep for 6 minutes. Add mint and steep 6 more minutes. Add sugar and lemon juice. Add enough water and ice to make a total of 1½ quarts. (NOTE: When doubling recipe, add only 1 cup of sugar and juice of 3 lemons.)

TENNIS ROUND ROBIN BRUNCH
Serves 8

Transfusions

Assorted Cheese Board with Clusters of Grapes and Crackers *

Cool as Cucumber-Shrimp with Pineapple and Hard-Cooked Eggs *

Hot Garlic Bread **

Chocolate Macaroons *

Coffee or Tea

It is always great fun to play tennis and invite people back for a meal. Since it can be very hot in July, a good idea is to play tennis early. Eight is a perfect number for a round robin, so why not reserve your courts for ten in the morning and invite your guests back to your house for a terrific brunch. You will want a do-ahead meal which is light and cool. Chances are everyone will be thirsty and hungry after a hard game of tennis and you will want to serve a light drink and cheeses to nibble on as soon as you get to your house. This Cool as Cucumber-Shrimp dish will look elegant on a large round platter (or two smaller platters) and will be the highlight of your buffet table.

Table Setting

Hot weather and outdoor sports make this a perfect time to entertain casually. You probably have a few empty tennis cans which can serve as appropriate and unusual containers for the beautiful flowers from your garden. Don't forget to get prizes for the winner or winners of your tennis round robin. These can be wrapped and used on your serving table as part of the decorations and then presented after your delicious brunch. Your picnic table covered with a bright yellow paper tablecloth serves your buffet. Bright green paper napkins complete your gay color scheme. The only other things you need are forks!

*Do ahead
**Freeze

Transfusion

A delicious and refreshing drink, with or without alcohol. Very popular for tennis players after the game! Makes 1 serving.

1 jigger vodka or gin
3 jiggers grape juice
ginger ale

Combine vodka or gin with grape juice over ice cubes in a tall glass. Fill to top with ginger ale.

Assorted Cheese Board with Clusters of Grapes and Crackers

Make a trip to your cheese shop and ask them to recommend a few cheeses to serve eight people. Often the owners will be very gracious in helping you select a nice combination. They also usually give you little tasty samples! These stores have excellent and different crackers. Arrange your cheeses and grapes on a platter and remove from your refrigerator before you play tennis (you don't want to serve cold cheese). Add the crackers and cold grapes just before serving.

Cool as Cucumber-Shrimp with Pineapple and Hard-Cooked Eggs

Wait until your guests see how clever you are with the lovely looking arrangement of these refreshing and delicious morsels of food. It is all so easy, and the whole tray (or trays) can be put in your refrigerator, covered with clear plastic wrap hours ahead. Serves 8.

2 cans (20 ounces each) sliced pineapple, chilled
4 cups cucumber slices
2 pounds shrimp, cooked and cleaned
12 hard-cooked eggs, shelled and carefully sliced
2 quarts torn assorted greens
2 packages salad dressing (such as Hidden Valley Ranch), prepared as directed, or your own favorite creamy dressing

Drain pineapple. Divide and stack pineapple in center of two round serving plates. Cover the remaining surface of both serving plates with greens. Arrange shrimp and cucumber around pineapple on both plates covering most of the lettuce. Use six rows (one egg per row) of sliced eggs for each platter, starting from the outer edges of pineapples out to edge of platters. Dribble some of the dressing over stacks of pineapple and put the rest in a small serving bowl.

Hot Garlic Bread

My very good friend always serves this, and the rest of us agree it is the very best recipe for garlic bread. Serves 8.

1 long, thin loaf of Italian bread
1 stick butter (½ cup)
½ teaspoon garlic powder
1 tablespoon grated Parmesan cheese
1 tablespoon dried parsley

Melt butter and add garlic powder, Parmesan cheese and parsley. Using a sharp knife, slice bread into very thin slices (approximately ¼-inch thick), but do not cut completely through the bottom. Use a small paint brush or pastry brush to spread the melted butter mixture on both sides of the slices of bread. Wrap securely with aluminum foil. Freeze. Thaw to room temperature the day of your brunch. Bake, still wrapped in the foil, at 300° for 20 minutes. Serve hot.

Chocolate Macaroons

This is the best cookie. It is light and chewy and I cannot tell you how long they keep, since they are always gobbled right up. My mother made these for us for years when we were growing up and we loved them. They still taste as good. Easy to make. Yield about 45 macaroons.

2 egg whites
1 cup sugar
⅛ teaspoon salt
½ teaspoon vanilla
1½ cups shredded coconut
1½ squares unsweetened chocolate, melted

Beat egg whites until stiff. Fold in sugar and salt; beat again until smooth. Add vanilla, then stir in coconut and chocolate. Drop by scant teaspoonsful on baking sheet. Bake at 275° for 20 minutes.

FOURTH OF JULY WEEKEND BRUNCH
Serves 18

Sangria *
Zucchini and Italian Sausage Quiche *
Red, White and Blue Star Salad Mold *
Tiny Rolls *
Watermelon Basket *
Yummy Chocolate Nougat Bars **

There is no better time to entertain than the Fourth of July, since everyone is in a festive mood and scheduled activities go on all weekend. A brunch invitation will be a welcome treat for friends and their weekend guests. The menu has been planned so everything can be done ahead; this way you can participate in any of the weekend activities knowing your brunch is ready to serve. A patriotic occasion such as this is a perfect time to present your special Red, White and Blue Star Salad Mold!

Table Setting

This is one of the easiest and most enjoyable brunches because you can really have fun with the theme. You might start with a flag-red cloth on your picnic table and crisscross red, white and blue streamers in the middle of the table. You can also use streamers for a large bow tied to a pretty basket for the tiny rolls. The decorative Watermelon Basket entwined with ivy and heaped with icy fruit can be your centerpiece. It will be a delicious end to your meal when you bring out your dessert bowls and Yummy Chocolate Nougat Bars. To further follow your theme, use white wicker plate holders with dark blue paper plates, red, white and blue napkins and heavy white plastic forks. Remember that anything goes; from varied Fourth of July paper decorations to pinwheels and sparklers.

*Do ahead
**Freeze

Sangria

This Sangria base is very good for a crowd, and what you have left-over will keep indefinitely in closed jars in your refrigerator. Make this as far in advance as you wish.

5 lemons
4 oranges
2 limes
3 pounds sugar
  (6¾ cups)
2 quarts water

In a large pan or kettle add 2 quarts water, wedges and slices from 3 lemons, 2 oranges and the 2 limes. After this comes to a boil, slowly add the three pounds of sugar, stirring constantly until the sugar is dissolved. Continue cooking, stirring occasionally, for 30 minutes, or until syrupy. Mash and squeeze remaining fruit into the hot syrup and let stand. Chill. Each pitcher serves 5 or 6 drinks.

To make 1 pitcher of sangria:

⅔ cup base
1 fifth red wine
1 large orange (gar-
  nish), sliced
3 lemons (garnish),
  sliced
1 cup carbonated water
1 tray ice cubes

Combine base, wine and 1 tray of ice cubes in large glass pitcher and mix thoroughly. Garnish with thin orange and lemon slices. Top with carbonated water and gently stir. Serve in large wineglasses with 2 ice cubes and 2 very thin slices of orange and lemon.

Zucchini and Italian Sausage Quiche

The combination of zucchini and sweet sausage is different and delicious. There is plenty of zucchini around in July and the sweet sausage is very light in this. Since you may wish to make this great quiche on an occasion calling for one pie, the recipe below is for one pie. Cut each pie into six generous portions. To serve 18, triple the recipe.

1 9 or 10-inch frozen
  unbaked pie shell
¾ pound zucchini,
  shredded (2 cups)
4 tablespoons (½ stick)
  butter
½ pound sweet Italian
  sausage
1 cup shredded Swiss
  cheese (4 ounces)
4 eggs
1 cup milk

½ cup heavy cream
¼ cup grated Parmesan
  cheese
½ teaspoon salt
dash pepper

Prepare and bake piecrust according to label directions. Use a 9 or 10 inch pie plate or fluted quiche dish. Sauté zucchini in 2 tablespoons of the butter in a large skillet for 5 minutes. Remove to colander to drain. Remove casing from sausages and cook in remaining 2 tablespoons butter in same skillet until pink disappears. Drain on paper towel. Spread zucchini evenly onto bottom of pastry shell; sprinkle sausage and Swiss cheese over zucchini. Beat eggs lightly in a large bowl. Add milk, heavy cream, cheese, salt and pepper; blend well. Pour into pastry shell. Bake at 450° for 15 minutes, then lower to 350° and bake for 15 minutes longer. Cool, then refrigerate. One hour before cooking, let stand at room temperature. Reheat at 350° for 30 minutes.

Red, White and Blue Star Salad Mold

It is always nice to have something different that fits a special occasion. This salad tastes as good as it looks. The recipe calls for a star mold, and you will need to triple it to serve 18. You may wish to make this in a 13½ × 8¾ × 1¾-inch pyrex flat dish, which is perfect for this recipe tripled . . . that is in case you cannot get three star-shaped molds. Serves 6.

2 packages strawberry-flavored gelatin
1 package (10 ounces) frozen strawberries, thawed
½ cup dairy sour cream
1½ cups miniature marshmallows
½ cup heavy cream, whipped
1 cup blueberries

Dissolve gelatin in 2 cups boiling water; chill until thickened. Mix in thawed strawberries. Pour into 5-cup star mold. Mixture will fill mold about halfway. Chill until set. Combine sour cream and marshmallows. Mix well. Fold in whipped cream. Unmold gelatin. Frost top with marshmallow mixture; cover with blueberries. Refrigerate covered.

Tiny Rolls

Go to your bakery or supermarket for these.

3 dozen tiny rolls
butter

Slit and butter rolls. Wrap in aluminum foil securely and freeze. Take out of freezer morning of brunch and heat if you wish.

Watermelon Basket

This looks delicious and beautiful. You should use this as a centerpiece since it looks so pretty. Everyone can admire it while they are helping themselves to brunch and will be dying to have some for dessert. There is a lot of cutting. Do this at least the day before. Serves 18-25.

1 cup sugar
1 cup water
1 pineapple, peeled
    and cut into chunks
1 watermelon
½ pound grapes, seed-
    less or pitted
1 small cantaloupe, cut
    in balls
1 small honeydew
    melon, cut in balls
1 pound Bing cherries,
    pitted
5 oranges, sectioned
1 pint strawberries
1 pint blueberries
1½ cups Cointreau

Boil sugar and water 5 minutes; cool. Add pineapple; soak a few hours or overnight. Cut watermelon lengthwise from each end, leaving a 2-inch section in center to form handle of basket. Scoop out red pulp, leaving shell 1-inch thick; scallop cut edges. Cube 2 cups watermelon; combine with drained pineapple and remaining fruit; arrange in "basket"; add Cointreau and some pineapple syrup. Set basket on lettuce-lined tray. Refrigerate until ready to serve.

Yummy Chocolate Nougat Bars

This recipe is very easy and freezes well. These nougat bars are so full of calories it might not be a good idea to mention all the ingredients! Makes approximately 60 squares.

3 tablespoons butter
½ package Sour Cream
    Chocolate Fudge
    Cake Mix or any
    packaged cake mix
    (2 cups)
1½ cups miniature
    marshmallows
1 small (6-ounce)
    package semisweet
    chocolate pieces
1 can flaked coconut
1 cup broken nuts
1 can (14 ounces)
    sweetened con-
    densed milk

Melt butter in dish 13½ × 8¾ × 1¾ inches in 350° oven. Sprinkle cake mix evenly in dish then layer rest of ingredients in order. Bake at 325° for 25 minutes. Cool. Cut in small squares.

AUGUST

POOL PARTY BRUNCH
Serves 4

> Pimm's Cup
> Strawberry Omelet
> Nova Scotia Salmon and Cream Cheese *
> Toasted Bagels or English Muffins
> Coffee or Tea

If you are lucky enough to own or have access to a pool, discover the fun of entertaining at brunch. Your guests can be invited for late morning, and after a swim you can bet they will be ready for a refreshing drink and a delicious meal. Think how delightfully surprised your guests will be when they are served a fluffy omelet with fresh strawberries instead of the traditional foods cooked on a grill. You are sure to get praise for your unique menu! There is nothing as relaxing as lingering over a good meal chatting with friends and enjoying the sun.

Table Setting

Informality is the keynote here. Use your pretty and colorful placemats and napkins. You have probably been tempted to buy some of the beautiful luncheon plates which are decorated with fruit, birds or flowers; this is a great opportunity to show them off. Tiny bouquets of seasonal flowers at each setting will serve instead of a centerpiece at your umbrella table. The salmon, cream cheese and toasted bagels or English muffins can be placed attractively on a serving dish with lots of fresh dill to be passed around the table.

*Do ahead

Pimm's Cup

The numbers 1, 2 or 3 are always designated on the bottle of Pimm's Cup. The number indicates the liquor used as the base of the drink. Buy the Pimm's Cup that appeals to you. Chill. Mix with equal parts cold lemon soda. Float a sliced cucumber on top or make a finger-size swizzle stick from a slice of cucumber. If you have pewter mugs or glasses, by all means use them.

Strawberry Omelet

To make a good omelet is not difficult, but it requires practice and concentration. Practice an omelet a few times on your family before including one in your menu for guests. Your guests will think you are a genius for serving this and it looks terrific.

**1 pint fresh strawber-
  ries, hulled and
  sliced
(Save a few sliced
  strawberries for gar-
  nish)
½ cup sugar
8 eggs
½ teaspoon salt
dash pepper
2 tablespoons butter
dairy sour cream
watercress for garnish**

Combine sliced strawberries and sugar in small bowl and refrigerate. Break eggs into bowl; add salt and pepper. Beat briskly with fork just until yolks and whites are mixed. Place a large skillet over high heat. When skillet is sizzling hot, put in butter. Stir it around quickly with fork to coat bottom and sides of pan. Do not let butter brown. Pour in the eggs all at once. Stir eggs rapidly with a circular motion, using the flat of the fork; at the same time shake the pan to and fro over the heat. Stir just until free liquid begins to set. Let stand about 2 or 3 seconds. Shake the pan. The omelet should move freely and be ready to roll. Spoon strawberry mixture on omelet. Lift the side nearest the skillet handle, fold ⅓ of omelet over center. As you tilt the pan over the platter, let the omelet roll out onto it. Top the folded omelet with dollops of sour cream. Arrange sliced strawberries and watercress around omelet.

Nova Scotia Salmon and Cream Cheese

Go to the delicatessen department of your favorite supermarket and get their smoked salmon. The best around us is a Vita product called Nova Salmon, a real treat. It comes sliced, and this can be arranged on a platter with the cream cheese and lots of fresh dill and lemon wedges. Try your local cheese shop for fresh cream cheese; they may not always have it, but you will find it absolutely delicious.

**½ pound cream cheese
½ pound sliced salmon**

**fresh dill
lemon wedges**

Bagels or English Muffins

We use the toasted onion or plain Thomas' English muffins around here and love them. There are all kinds of bagels which are great, just split, toast and butter them. Make sure you have more than one whole one per person!

BRUNCH ON A BOAT
Serves 6

Bullshots

**One Large Wedge Cheese
and Party Bread ***

**Cold Artichokes with
Hollandaise Sauce ***

Hot Vichyssoise in Mugs *

Ham and Cheese Sandwiches on Buns *

Vanilla Brownies **

Coffee *

Let's assume you have been invited aboard someone's boat for a day trip and you have gaily volunteered to bring brunch for six hungry people. To really make a hit, the secret is to plan ahead and go through the entire menu in your head as to exactly how and with what everyone will eat so you do not forget a thing. Everything will be served with ease! It involves disposable flatware, plates, glasses, cups, napkins and a large picnic hamper. You need special containers, as the hot must be hot and the cold, cold. Don't forget a large, thick plastic bag for trash. You need plenty of food; be ready to offer the wedge of cheese as soon as people arrive at the boat.

Table Setting

Since there will be no formal table setting, pack your hamper so it will be appealing to the eye. Use a bright checkered cloth to line your hamper, folding it over the contents when it is full. Disposable utensils in a complementary color will add sparkle to your hamper. The gay colors will have to suffice for decorations — there is no place for them on a boat!

*Do ahead
**Freeze

Bullshots

You can make this on the boat. Just have plenty of ice and plenty of ingredients. Makes 6 drinks.

12 jiggers vodka or gin
3 cans consommé or
** beef bouillon**
Worcestershire sauce
salt
pepper
1 lime

In each mug, put ice, 2 jiggers vodka or gin, and fill with consommé. Season with Worcestershire sauce, salt, pepper and a squeeze of lime. Stir well.

One Large Wedge (3 Pounds) Cheese and Party Bread

Either use your delicatessen department in your supermarket or a cheese shop and get a wedge of your favorite cheese. Make sure you have an appropriate cheese knife. Use any of the party breads, but it might be easier to use a loaf where the slices are small.

Cold Artichokes With Hollandaise Sauce

Everyone will think you are so clever for bringing something this elegant for your hamper. This can all be done ahead and chilled. Serves 6.

6 large artichokes
olive oil
½ teaspoon garlic
** powder**

Wash artichokes in cold water. Cut off stem so it has a flat bottom surface to stand on. Pull off the outer woody leaves around the bottom. Hold the artichoke on its side and cut off the upper third, removing the prickly tips of the leaves. Use a melonball scoop or a small spoon to remove the center and the fuzzy core. Pour into a large pan with a lid about one inch of water; add oil and garlic powder. Place the artichokes close together, bottom-side-down, in the pan. Cook, covered for 24 minutes. Refrigerate. Just before leaving, fill centers with Hollandaise Sauce and securely wrap in plastic wrap.

Hollandaise Sauce

6 egg yolks
4 tablespoons lemon
** juice**
¼ teaspoon salt
1⅓ cups butter

Place yolks, lemon juice and salt in blender container; cover and turn to high speed for 4 seconds. Remove cover and add the melted butter in a thin, steady stream. Sauce will be done in 30 seconds. Refrigerate.

Hot Vichyssoise in Mugs

It will be nice to have something warm out on a boat. If you really have a hot hot day, then do not heat — have it cold instead. Serves 6.

2 leeks
2 tablespoons butter
1½ cups thin sliced
   potatoes
1 can chicken broth
2 teaspoons sugar
½ teaspoon salt
¼ teaspoon pepper
1 cup milk
1 cup heavy cream

Remove the green tops from the leeks and slice the white part into thin slices. Using a saucepan, sauté in the butter for 5 minutes, then add the potatoes and chicken broth. Cook uncovered over medium heat for about 25 minutes or until potatoes are tender. Put half the mixture in blender and mix. Repeat with the other half. Pour each half, after mixing, back into the saucepan. Add the rest of the ingredients, heat and then put in thermos. Serve as hot as the thermos will keep it. It is equally good chilled.

Ham and Cheese Sandwiches on Buns

A good ham and cheese sandwich is a perfect choice for this trip. Just buy good and fresh buns and good ham. Make more than one sandwich per person, since there will be lots of time for eating!

Vanilla Brownies

This recipe is so good you can serve this on any occasion. It has got to be the best of the best. Makes about 50 brownies. You may not need them all for six people.

⅔ cup butter
1 pound light brown
   sugar
3 eggs
2⅔ cups sifted flour
2½ teaspoons baking
   powder
½ teaspoon salt
1 large (12-ounce)
   package semisweet
   chocolate morsels
1 cup chopped pecans

Melt butter in large saucepan. Add sugar and blend well. Let cool approximately 10 minutes. Beat in eggs, one at a time. Add rest of ingredients and mix well. Spread into greased pan 15½ × 10½ inches. Bake at 350° for 25-30 minutes.

GOLF WIDOWS' BRUNCH ON A MEMBER-GUEST WEEKEND
Serves 8

Orange Sherbet Blossoms
Asparagus-Leek Soup *
Chef's Salad *
Bread Sticks *
Peach Shortcake *
Iced Tea *

When your husband announces he has signed up for a member-guest golf tournament all sorts of wild things race through your mind. For instance, you know that despite the evening partying, you and the other wives will be left to entertain yourselves during the day. Brunch will be perfect, since the men will leave early to tee off. Your guests will all be women, so you can plan the menu without considering men's hearty appetites. This do-ahead menu will leave you plenty of time with your guests. The gals will feel special being entertained at their own party and will surely compliment you for your ability to entertain without spending much time in the kitchen.

Table Setting

A brunch for ladies only is a perfect opportunity to set up two bridge tables on your porch, where you can enjoy the fresh air and eat in comfort. The often-forgotten first course is served from an elegant soup tureen set up on your tea cart next to your bridge tables. You can use your delicate Madeira bridge cloths and matching napkins. Small silver bowls with flowers will enhance your best china and silver. Frosty ice tea glasses and cut-glass dishes holding bread sticks and salad dressings will complete the picture.

*Do ahead
**Freeze

Orange Sherbet Blossoms

This easy-to-prepare drink is a very special treat. Use a pretty glass pitcher and pour into old fashioned, champagne or any nice glasses. Do half of this recipe at one time in your blender and pour into pitcher then repeat. Makes 8 drinks.

2 pints orange sherbet,
  softened
8 jiggers gin or vodka
4 tablespoons lemon
  juice
2 cups crushed ice
4 thin slices orange,
  halved for garnish

Place half of ingredients except orange slices in a blender and turn to high speed until blended. Empty into pitcher and repeat. Pour from pitcher into glasses and garnish with ½ orange slice.

Asparagus-Leek Soup

This is delicious and is so easy. Just heat and serve. Makes 8 servings.

2 packages frozen cut
  asparagus
1½ cups boiling water
2 envelopes leek soup
  mix
6 cups milk
½ teaspoon pepper
salt to taste
sour cream
chopped chives

Cook the frozen asparagus in the boiling water until it is tender. Pour the cooked asparagus, including the water, into the blender and whirl until smooth. Add the leek soup mix, 3 cups milk and the pepper. Blend. Pour into a pan and refrigerate. When ready to serve, add rest of milk (3 cups) and heat. Add salt. Pour soup into soup tureen and serve from porch. Serve in pretty dishes with a dollop of sour cream and the chives floating on top. Pass bread sticks.

Chef's Salad

Ladies love this salad. To make this a real do-ahead dish, prepare individual plates or bowls in the morning and cover with plastic wrap and refrigerate. Just uncover and serve. Serves 8.

1 garlic clove, halved
  (optional)
2 heads iceberg lettuce
  or romaine
2 cups thin strips
  cooked chicken or
  turkey
1 package (8 ounces)
  sliced Swiss cheese,
  cut in thin strips
1 package (12 ounces)
  sliced cooked ham,
  cut in thin strips
4 medium tomatoes,
  cut in wedges

4 hard-cooked eggs,
  quartered
classic French dressing
Russian dressing

If you like, rub bowls or plates with garlic clove and discard garlic. Into bowls or plates, tear lettuce into bite-size pieces. On lettuce, divide and arrange chicken or turkey, Swiss cheese, ham, tomato and egg wedges. Let guests help themselves to either of the dressings at their tables.

Bread Sticks

Your bakery should have nice ones. These are ideal for a ladies' brunch; just make sure you order plenty.

Peach Shortcake

Peaches are in season. What a delicious way to end a great brunch. Serves 8.

4 cups sliced peaches, sprinkled with lemon juice & ⅓ cup sugar
¼ cup sugar
1¾ cups all-purpose flour
½ cup shortening
⅓ cup milk
1 egg
1 tablespoon baking powder
1 teaspoon grated lemon peel
¾ teaspoon salt
butter, softened
1 cup heavy cream, whipped

Preheat oven to 450°. Grease a 9-inch round cake pan. Into medium bowl, measure ¼ cup sugar and next 7 ingredients. With mixer at medium speed, beat mixture until well combined and a soft dough forms. Pat dough evenly into pan. Bake 15 minutes or until golden. Invert shortcake onto platter; with long sharp knife, split hot shortcake horizontally. Spread cut surfaces with butter. Place bottom half on serving plate and cover with half of peaches; top with other cake half; spoon remaining peaches over top. Refrigerate. When ready to serve, spread whipped cream over peaches and garnish with a few slices of peaches.

Iced Tea

My family would love to have this every day in the summer. Serves 8.

Steep 5 tea bags in 5 cups of boiling water for 5 minutes. Add the juice of 2 lemons and ¾ cup sugar. When sugar is dissolved, add two trays of ice. Pour into tall iced tea glasses and garnish with sprigs of mint.

SEPTEMBER

LABOR DAY BRUNCH FOR SUMMER COTTAGE FRIENDS

Serves 6

Company Bloody Marys *
Cheese Oven Omelet
Sausage Patties *
Sliced Tomatoes *
Blueberry Muffins * *
Coffee

As your vacation draws to an end, you will want to get together with summer friends before you all go home. Labor Day weekend is a perfect time to do it. With summer windup activities going on all day, a brunch party will get Saturday, Sunday or Monday off to a good start. Living is casual at lakes and beaches, so your menu should reflect this easygoing style. This will be your last opportunity to be with the friends who have been summer companions. There will be lots to talk about — happy summer memories, winter reunions and plans for next summer.

Table Setting

Plan the setting of your brunch for a comfortable place on your dock, patio or deck. It should be served buffet-style so guests can help themselves to your pitcher of good drinks and to hearty food as they want it. When setting your table, use what is available from nature as a centerpiece. A cheerful bunch of wildflowers, a pretty jar of sea glass (colored pieces of glass washed up on the beach), or artfully arranged shells will all be appropriate. Whatever you have as far as dishes and silver will do just fine. You can be sure no one expects fine tableware!

*Do ahead
**Freeze

Company Bloody Marys

This recipe makes about 8 servings.

2 cans (18 ounces each)
   tomato juice (4½
   cups)
1 cup vodka
2 teaspoons Worcester-
   shire sauce
½ teaspoon salt
¼ teaspoon coarsely
   ground pepper
few dashes hot pepper
   sauce
ice cubes
2 limes, quartered
   lengthwise

In large pitcher, combine first 6 ingredients. Cover and refrigerate if made
ahead. Pour over ice cubes in highball
glasses. Squeeze a lime wedge into each
glass; stir.

Cheese Oven Omelet

*This is so easy. Just have your cheese shredded beforehand. You will be
free to chat with your friends, since this goes in the oven. Serves 6.*

10 eggs
1 cup milk
½ teaspoon seasoned
   salt
1½ cups shredded
   Cheddar or
   mozzarella cheese
   (about 6 ounces)
1 tablespoon instant
   minced onion

Heat oven to 325°. Beat eggs, milk and
seasoned salt. Stir in cheese and onion.
Pour into greased baking dish,
11½×7½×1½ or 8×8×2 inches. Bake
uncovered 40 to 45 minutes or until
omelet is set and top is golden brown.

Sausage Patties

*Buy a package of frozen, fully-cooked patties and follow directions. If
you wish to do them ahead, cook as directed and wrap in aluminum foil.
Refrigerate. Just pop them in the oven to heat with the muffins.*

Sliced Tomatoes

This is a perfect time of the year for plenty of delicious garden tomatoes. Just slice and arrange on a plate and refrigerate.

Blueberry Muffins

You may wish to buy a package mix, which is very easy. If you do not have muffin tins, try to find the disposable ones. Whichever you choose, they all freeze well. This recipe makes 12 muffins.

¾ cup fresh or frozen
   unsweetened
   blueberries
2 cups all-purpose
   flour
½ cup sugar
1 tablespoon baking
   powder
½ teaspoon salt
1 egg
1 cup milk
¼ cup salad oil

Heat oven to 400°. Grease twelve 2½-inch muffin-pan cups. In large bowl, mix flour and next 3 ingredients with fork. In small bowl, with fork, beat egg slightly; stir in milk, blueberries and oil. Add egg mixture to flour mixture all at once; with spoon, stir just until flour is moistened. (Batter will be lumpy.) Spoon batter into muffin-pan cups. Bake 20-25 minutes.

A NEW BABY CELEBRATION
Serves 8

Champagne with Peach
Cucumber Pinwheel Sandwiches*
Deviled Eggs Wrapped in Ham Casserole*
Heavenly Cheese Salad Mold*
Tomato Wedges*
Celebration Cake*
Coffee or Tea

You have had a baby! September is a beautiful month for the baby's special day. Invite relatives and close friends to your house for a celebration brunch. You can pop your casserole in the oven and it can heat while the proud father is serving champagne! It will be a busy morning, and everyone will appreciate a lovely tray of cucumber pinwheel sandwiches with the champagne.

Table Setting
For this joyous occasion use a white damask cloth with pink or blue linen napkins, your polished silver and pretty china. A delicate floral centerpiece of babies' breath and sweetheart roses will look lovely in a crystal bowl. Display your baby's celebration cake on your sideboard for everyone to admire. Don't forget to have someone take pictures — this is an occasion to remember.

*Do ahead
**Freeze

Champagne With Peach
With peaches in season, this adds an extra touch to the champagne.

Peel and halve fresh peaches, allowing one-half peach for each guest. Place peach half in a long-stemmed champagne glass. Fill to top with icy champagne and serve, giving each guest a spoon.

Cucumber Pinwheel Sandwiches

These are light and easy to do. These are best if done the day before serving. The fresher the bread the easier to do. Yield 30-36.

1 regular-sized loaf
   white bakery bread,
   sliced horizontally
   (by bakery)
½ large package (8
   ounces) cream
   cheese, softened
1½ unpeeled cucum-
   bers, grated
1 small onion, grated
salt to taste
mayonnaise

Mix cucumber and onion, drain well through cheesecloth, squeezing out most of the liquid. Mix this into the cream cheese. Add salt and enough mayonnaise to make a spread. Remove all crusts from bread. Lightly roll each slice with a rolling pin to help prevent cracking. Spread bread to edges with filling. Starting at one end, roll tightly, jelly-roll fashion. Wrap rolls securely with waxed paper like a party favor and twist ends. Refrigerate. To serve, cut rolls into ½-inch slices.

Deviled Eggs Wrapped In Ham Casserole

A lovely company dish. This can easily be done a day or two ahead of serving. Serves 8.

Deviled Eggs:

8 hard-cooked eggs
1½ teaspoons finely
   chopped onion
½ teaspoon dry mus-
   tard

½ teaspoon salt
3 tablespoons mayon-
   naise
1 teaspoon Worcester-
   shire sauce

Cheese Sauce:

3 tablespoons butter
2 teaspoons chopped
   onion
3 tablespoons flour
2¾ cups milk
1½ cups grated Ched-
   dar cheese
½ teaspoon salt

8 medium-thin slices ham
3 packages (10 ounces
   each) frozen
   chopped spinach,
   cooked and drained
1½ cups crushed
   cornflakes
¼ cup melted butter

Arrange spinach in a pretty oval or rectangular baking dish (approximately 7×11 inches). Slice hard-cooked eggs in half, lengthwise. Scoop out yolks and mash with next five ingredients. Fill whites with stuffing and place 2 halves together to make one whole egg. Wrap one ham slice around each egg. Arrange over spinach. In a saucepan melt 3 tablespoons butter, add onion and simmer 5 minutes. Add flour then milk, stirring until sauce thickens. Stir in cheese, season with salt. Mix well, making sure cheese has melted. Pour sauce over deviled eggs and refrigerate. Sprinkle buttered cornflakes on top and bake at 350° for 20-30 minutes until bubbly hot.

Heavenly Cheese Salad Mold

This always brings raves. The flavor is marvelous and it is so easy to prepare. You can make this a few days before serving. Serves 8.

1 package lemon flavored gelatin (3 ounces)
1 cup boiling water
¾ cup pineapple juice
1 tablespoon lemon juice
1¼ cups drained crushed pineapple
1 cup (¼ pound) shredded sharp Cheddar cheese
1 cup heavy cream, whipped
lettuce

Dissolve gelatin in water; add juices. Chill until slightly thickened. Fold in crushed pineapple, cheese and whipped cream and pour into 1½-quart mold. Chill. Unmold on lettuce.

Tomato Wedges

At this time of the year, it is hard to plan a meal without using delicious fresh tomatoes. Use a pretty cut-glass bowl heaped with peeled or unpeeled bright red wedges.

Place whole tomato on a fork and submerge in boiling water for approximately 15 seconds. Remove and run cold water over tomato and using a sharp paring knife, pull back skin. Cut tomatoes into wedges. Sprinkle with fresh basil or dill. Refrigerate.

Celebration Cake

Order a lovely and simply decorated cake from your bakery with the baby's name and birthdate. You may request a cake with a space for a small container of fresh flowers in the middle. Of course, you may be the one who has to provide the container and the flowers!

COMMITTEE KICK-OFF BRUNCH
Serves 12

Cranberry Punch Bowl
Bacon and Eggs Supreme *
Spectacular Fruit Salad *
Tiny Marmalade Biscuits *
Peanut Blossom Cookies **
Coffee

This is your year to head a committee. After a lazy summer, suddenly fall arrives and with it your responsibilities to the Girl Scouts, Red Cross, a hospital service organization or a civic committee. You will find people will look forward to their first get-together if it starts off with a different twist — discover brunch for business as well as social affairs! This is an informal and friendly way for people who will be working together to meet for the first time.

Table Setting

One of the first signs of fall is its colors. A crockery bean pot overflowing with black-eyed susans will look autumn-like in the center of your table. Wildflowers are abundant, so while you are out picking the black-eyed susans for your centerpiece, gather great bunches and place them around your house for your guests to enjoy. A pale gold cloth and matching napkins, a bright pottery casserole dish and pottery plates will complete your color scheme. This is a good opportunity to use your stainless flatware. Use your imagination; the punch can be served from pottery pitchers or a large crock as well as from a punch bowl.

*Do ahead
**Freeze

Cranberry Punch Bowl

This is easy to prepare and tastes wonderful. The following recipe makes 24 drinks.

2 quarts cranberry
   juice
1 can (6 ounces) frozen
   orange juice concen-
   trate, undiluted
¼ cup sugar

1 pint vodka
2 bottles (7 ounces
   each) carbonated
   water
orange and lemon
   slices

Combine cranberry juice, orange juice and sugar in a punch bowl and stir until sugar is dissolved. Stir in vodka. Add a large block of ice or lots of ice cubes. Pour carbonated water over punch. Garnish with orange and lemon slices.

Bacon and Eggs Supreme

This tasty dish will easily serve 12 hungry people and can be done a day or two in advance.

¼ cup butter
¼ cup flour
1 cup cream
1 cup milk
¼ teaspoon each:
　thyme, marjoram,
　basil
¼ cup chopped parsley
1 pound sharp Cheddar
　cheese, grated
1½ dozen hard-cooked
　eggs, sliced in half
　lengthwise
1 pound bacon, cooked
　and crumbled
2 cups bread crumbs
½ cup butter

Melt ¼ cup butter in a medium-size saucepan. Add flour, milk and cream, stirring until sauce thickens. Stir in herbs and cheese. Mix well, making sure cheese has melted. Arrange eggs in a greased large pottery baking dish (approximately 3-quart size). If your dish is deep, you can slice your eggs vertically with an egg slicer so you will have more pieces. Layer bacon, sauce and buttered bread crumbs on top. Refrigerate. Bake uncovered for 30 minutes at 350°.

Spectacular Fruit Salad

This recipe came from my aunt, who is a fabulous cook. The dressing goes well with any fruit salad. Use any proportions of the fruits mentioned or make substitutions.

Dressing:
⅓ cup sugar
1 teaspoon toasted
　sesame seeds
1 teaspoon salt
1 teaspoon dry mustard
4 tablespoons vinegar
1 cup salad oil
1 teaspoon paprika
1 teaspoon grated
　onion

mango, peeled and cut
　in thin strips
orange, peeled and
　sliced crosswise
pineapple, peeled and
　cut into small
　chunks
seedless grapes, cut in
　half
bibb lettuce
watercress

Mix ingredients for dressing in a jar. Cover, shake well and refrigerate. Place fruit, watercress and lettuce in a bowl in refrigerator. Shake dressing and pour over salad. Carefully toss and serve.

Tiny Marmalade Biscuits

Everyone enjoys these light, colorful and easily prepared biscuits. You can bake these before your guests arrive and just reheat before serving. Makes 3 dozen small biscuits.

½ cup orange mar-
  malade
2 tablespoons soft but-
  ter
2 cups Bisquick baking
  mix
½ cup cold water

Heat oven to 425°. Mix marmalade and butter; spread in 8×8×2-inch baking pan. Stir baking mix and water to a soft dough. Gently smooth dough into a ball on floured cloth-covered board. Knead 5 times. Roll into 8-inch square; place on marmalade-butter mixture in pan. Pat evenly into corners; cut into 36 squares. Bake 15-20 minutes. Invert pan on serving plate. Biscuits will break off into small, bite-size pieces. Serve warm.

Peanut Blossom Cookies

A favorite with all ages. Very easy to make. Makes about 45 cookies.

1¾ cups all-purpose
  flour
½ cup sugar
½ cup brown sugar
1 teaspoon soda
½ teaspoon salt
½ cup solid shortening
½ cup chunky or
  smooth peanut but-
  ter
2 tablespoons milk
1 teaspoon vanilla
1 egg
Hershey chocolate kis-
  ses

Preheat oven to 375°. Combine all ingredients except chocolate kisses in a large mixing bowl. Mix at low speed until a dough forms. Shape dough into balls using a rounded teaspoonful of dough. Roll balls in additional white sugar and place on ungreased cookie sheet. Bake for 10-12 minutes. As soon as they come out of the oven place a chocolate kiss in the middle of each cookie.

OCTOBER

FOOTBALL TAILGATE BRUNCH
Serves 4

Red Wine Spritzers
Split Pea Soup **
Raw Broccoli and Dip *
Baked Chicken Pieces *
Tiny Cheese Sandwiches *
Special Brownies **
Coffee *

One of the best things about fall is a football game on a crisp October day. Make plans with a favorite couple to drive to the game and enjoy a tailgate brunch together. Make sure you leave plenty of time to enjoy your meal, as football games start promptly. The food should be easily transportable and should look as good when you unpack it as when you put it together. Chicken travels well, as does the rest of the menu. Your decor depends only on your imagination. Anything from silver candlesticks to paper plates is acceptable; I always strive for a happy medium. To me, being outdoors in the crisp air suggests using natural things. A little extra thought in packaging each item of the menu will make your brunch memorable. Pack your chicken and sandwiches in a flat wicker tray covered with a bright napkin and tie it all together with a pretty bow. You may even have some fabulous fabric scraps that will do the job gaily.

Table Setting

Color is the keynote for your tailgate. Mix and match bold colors and prints for your tablecloth, napkins, cups and plates. Just check your list carefully to make sure you have the right utensils for your menu. Since chicken is a little messy, make sure you include disposable moist towels. Your guests will know you have thought of everything when your husband pours the spritzers into wineglasses and you place a centerpiece of strawflowers on the tailgate.

*Do ahead
**Freeze

Wine Spritzers

This is a nice light drink. Makes approximately 10 drinks.

1 bottle red or white wine
1 large bottle club soda
ice

Fill glass with ice cubes. Pour equal amounts of wine and club soda to top of glass.

Split Pea Soup

This is worth the extra ingredients. Yield: 3½ quarts.

2 quarts water
2 cups dried green split
  peas
1 whole ham hock,
  split
10 peppercorns
3 carrots, cut into small
  pieces
½ cup chopped onion
2 cups chopped celery
2 tablespoons chopped
  parsley
1 cup milk
2 cups beef bouillon
salt to taste

Soak peas in 2 quarts of water overnight. Bring to boil in same water. Reduce heat, add ham hock and peppercorns; simmer covered for 1 hour. Press peas and liquid through a coarse sieve. To this mixture add carrots, onions, celery and parsley; cook until vegetables are tender. Add ham (removed from bone and shredded), milk and bouillon; simmer 20 minutes. Add salt to taste.

Raw Broccoli and Dip

This really looks nice when you serve it on a pretty dish. The broccoli looks so shiny and dark green. This is a little different for a vegetable dish and your guests will insist on this recipe. Very easy to prepare. Serves approximately 8 persons.

1 large bunch fresh
  broccoli
Marinade:
¼ cup cider or wine
  vinegar
¾ cup salad oil
2 cloves garlic, split
1 teaspoon sugar
2 teaspoons dill

Dip:
2 cups mayonnaise
1½ tablespoons curry
1 tablespoon ketchup
¼ teaspoon Worcester-
  shire sauce

Cut flowerettes from broccoli with 1-1½-inch stems. Split the large ones to make them bite-size. Combine ingredients for marinade in a jar and shake well. Put cut broccoli in a medium size baggie and pour over marinade. Tie baggie and refrigerate up to a day before serving. Mix ingredients for dip and refrigerate. Drain broccoli and serve with dip.

Baked Chicken Pieces

This is easy to do and tastes delicious. A trick I have learned is to wrap the cooked chicken securely in aluminum foil after cooking. Reheat just before leaving the house and place in a towel. This assures warm chicken for the tailgate picnic brunch. Serves 4, 2 pieces each.

1 whole chicken cut
  into 8 pieces
1½ sticks butter, melted
2 cups herb seasoned
  stuffing (such as
  Pepperidge Farm),
  crushed

Preheat oven to 400°. Dip chicken parts into melted butter. Coat pieces of chicken with crushed stuffing and place in a single layer in pan, skin-side-up. Bake, uncovered, 50-60 minutes.

Tiny Cheese Sandwiches

Purchase some packaged 2-inch square soft rolls. Split and butter. Fill with Swiss cheese, salt, pepper and lettuce.

Special Brownies

Very easy and a favorite with everyone. Freezes well. Yield 1½ dozen.

1 cup flour
1 cup sugar
¼ teaspoon salt
½ stick (4 tablespoons)
  butter
½ cup water
2 tablespoons cocoa
¼ cup liquid shorten-
  ing (vegetable oil)
¼ cup buttermilk or
  sour milk*
½ teaspoon baking
  soda
½ teaspoon vanilla
1 egg

Frosting:
½ stick (4 tablespoons)
  butter
2 tablespoons cocoa
3 tablespoons butter-
  milk or sour milk
½ box confectioners'
  sugar
½ cup chopped nuts

Sift and set aside flour, sugar and salt. Boil together the butter, water, cocoa and shortening. Pour the boiled chocolate mixture over the flour mixture and mix well. Add buttermilk, eggs, baking soda and vanilla. Mix well and pour into a greased and floured 9x9-inch pan. Bake at 400° for 15-20 minutes. While brownies are baking, boil margarine, cocoa and buttermilk. Add sifted confectioners' sugar, nuts and frost immediately out of the oven.

*To make sour milk: Add 1½ table-
spoons vinegar or lemon juice to 1 cup
milk. Let set for a few minutes.

A BRUNCH FOLLOWING THE HUNT
Serves 8

Hot Burgundy Bowl
Ale
Roasted Pecans **
Scrambled Eggs
Sautéed Kidneys
Bacon
Baked Bananas *
English Muffins
Marmalades
Coffee

Your friends are going on an early morning hunt and you have invited a few back for a hearty brunch. The air is crisp and there is much excitement surrounding the hunt. The Hot Burgundy Bowl and Roasted Pecans provide a chic beginning to an elegant English hunt menu. This classic brunch will draw raves from your friends and will surely become an annual event.

Table Setting

A bright red tablecloth, pewter and fine china create an English mood which will be enhanced by those of your guests who come in their "pinks." Pewter tankards of ale, heavy flatware and serving pieces, red napkins and white china set the stage for an English country meal. For your centerpiece, scatter brightly colored leaves in the center of your table and cross two riding crops on top. A black hunt cap in the middle and a low bouquet of full yellow chrysanthemums on each end will complete your brunch table.

*Do ahead
**Freeze

Hot Burgundy Bowl

The aroma of this drink fills the entire house and is fantastic. Everyone will be warmed up in no time at all. This will be especially nice served in a pewter bowl or pitcher. Makes about 12 punch cup servings.

1 bottle (⁴/₅ quart) Burgundy
1 cup sugar
2 lemons, thinly sliced
4 whole cloves
1 stick cinnamon
2 cups water

Pour water into a large pan. Add sugar, cloves and cinnamon and let this come to a boil. Then simmer for 5 minutes. Remove from heat and add lemons then steep for 10 minutes. Add wine, heat slowly to a boil and serve.

Ale

Have some cold good ale for those who are extra thirsty. Very appropriate served from pewter tankards.

Roasted Pecans

These have a hot-peppery taste and are quite different and good.

2 cups pecan halves
1½ tablespoons butter, melted
1 teaspoon salt
2 teaspoons soy sauce
⅛ teaspoon hot pepper sauce (Tabasco)

Preheat oven to 300°. In 8- or 9-inch cake pan, combine pecans and butter. Toast in oven 30 minutes, stirring occasionally. Add rest of ingredients and toss.

Scrambled Eggs

I always figure on 2 eggs per person when scrambling. I get best results when cooking over a medium heat and when I use a large spoon to turn eggs gently. You will probably want to do this in 2 large skillets. Serves 8.

16 fresh eggs
1¼ teaspoons salt
1 cup cream
1 stick (8 tablespoons) butter

Melt butter in a skillet over low heat. Break eggs into a bowl and add rest of ingredients. Beat lightly. Set burner to medium-low and add egg mixture. When eggs just begin to set, gently fold eggs over with a large spoon. They may be cooked to any degree of thickness you like. Eggs will set a bit more, from their own heat, after removal from the skillet. Do not overcook!

Sautéed Kidneys

My mother does these to perfection. My sisters and I always request this feast when we go to visit. The combination of sautéed kidneys and the bacon and bananas is really a treat. This recipe allows about 4 halves per serving. Have them washed and cleaned ahead of time. They do not take very long to cook. Serves 8.

2 pounds lamb kidneys
milk
flour

salt and pepper
butter

Split and devein kidneys. Use curved nail scissors to devein and to remove any fat. Heat skillet and add butter (enough to sauté kidneys.) Dip kidneys in milk, then into a mixture of flour and salt and pepper. Sauté kidneys in a skillet over medium heat 5-8 minutes, turning once during this time.

Bacon

A very good friend who used to be an airline stewardess said this was the way the hostesses were taught to cook bacon on planes years ago. I tried it and have been doing it her way ever since. Just make sure you don't forget it's in the oven!

Lay bacon slices on rack of bacon baker or on a rack set in a baking pan. Bake in a preheated 400° oven until done to your liking. About 10-15 minutes. Remove and place on a plate lined with paper towels.

Baked Bananas

These are the best and so easy. Allow 3 sections for each serving. Makes 8 servings.

6 bananas
2 tablespoons butter, melted
⅓ cup sugar
2 tablespoons lemon juice

Heat oven to 350°. Remove skins from bananas and cut in half crosswise and lengthwise (4 sections). Place in flat baking dish. Combine rest of ingredients and pour half the mixture over the bananas. Bake bananas for 10 minutes, then pour over rest of mixture and bake 10 more minutes.

English Muffins

The best kind to buy are the Thomas' English Muffins. Allow plenty of these for your guests. Just split with a fork, toast and butter.

Marmalades

Go to your gourmet shop or delicatessen and splurge on some really fine imported marmalades. Empty them into pretty dishes or keep them in their own pretty jars.

MONSTER BASH
Serves 10-12

Poisonous Punch
(Cider)

Transylvania Treats
(Doughnuts)

Ghoulish Goolash*
(Sloppy Joes)

Vulture Eggs*
(Deviled Eggs)

Monster Marvels*
(Taffy Apples)

A weekend morning brunch for pre-teenagers on Halloween will be perfect, since dad will be around to help with the fun and the guests will be free to trick or treat later in the day. Young people love to plan their own parties, and Halloween is tailor-made for children's fertile imaginations. As long as the guests will be old enough not to be afraid, let your child think up and help prepare the scary decorations and games. A very important part of this party is the decorations. Your child can make spiders with black pipe cleaners and suspend them with thread, he can cut bats out of construction paper and make skeletons from white paper. A black light shining on these as the guests enter will create a spooky atmosphere! Costumes are a must for the guests, and prizes should be awarded for the most unusual, prettiest, scariest, etc. It is a good idea to have a small prize or ribbon for each guest — you can always think of categories after you see the costumes.

Table Setting

For a group of this size, it is wise to use a folding table or a large picnic table. Set it up where there is plenty of space — in your basement or playroom. Cover it with orange fabric and suspend a witch piñata stuffed with candy over the center. Some black streamers will also be effective. Cardboard cut in the shape of gravestones and painted gray can be attached to the back of each child's chair with "Here lies Macky" or "Johnny" or "Karen" or "Amy" printed on them. These will make a big hit. Have a menu at each place or a large poster listing the foods the kids will be eating. They will love reading "Poisonous Punch," "Transylvania Treats," "Ghoulish Goolash," "Vulture Eggs," "Monster Marvels,"

*Do ahead

etc. Use Halloween paper plates, napkins and cups and plastic forks which you can buy in your local five-and-ten or stationery store. After the meal is over and the table is cleared, your guests can try to break the piñata. A plastic baseball bat or a broom handle can be used. Blindfold one child at a time and give each five chances to break the papier-maché witch — wait until you see the faces on the kids and hear the yells. They all think it is easy to smash the piñata — they do not realize that it is harder than it looks!

Poisonous Punch
(Cider)

Kids and adults love cider. This is a perfect time of the year to serve it. Just make sure you have space for lots of it in your refrigerator.

Transylvania Treats
(Doughnuts)

Purchase at a local special doughnut store or your supermarket.

Ghoulish Goolash
(Sloppy Joes)

This is a very big hit with kids. This will serve 12 hearty appetites.

2 pounds ground beef
12 sliced hamburger buns, buttered
2 cans (10½ ounces each) tomato soup
2 tablespoons prepared mustard
½ teaspoon salt

Wrap buns in aluminum foil and heat in 325° oven for 15 minutes. Brown beef in skillet. Stir in soup, mustard and salt. Simmer over low heat 10 minutes, stirring occasionally. Spoon into warm buns.

Vulture Eggs
(Deviled Eggs)

A tasty finger food, easily prepared. Serves 12.

12 hard-cooked eggs
¾ teaspoon salt
½ teaspoon pepper
¾ teaspoon dry mus-
  tard
6 tablespoons mayon-
  naise

Cut hard-cooked eggs in halves. Slip out yolks. Mash with fork. Mix in rest of ingredients. Refill whites with egg yolk mixture, heaping it up lightly. Top with a slice of pickle.

Monster Marvels
(Taffy Apples)

A special treat for a special occasion. Serves 12.

12 medium apples
3 cups sugar
¾ cup water
¼ teaspoon cream of
  tartar
¾ cup butter
1½ teaspoons vinegar
¾ cup cream

Place the sugar and water in a saucepan and heat until dissolved. Add the cream of tartar, butter, vinegar and cream. Cook, stirring constantly, to 290°, or to the soft-crack stage. Remove from heat. Dip each apple, held by a wooden skewer, into the boiled mixture and carefully place on a buttered plate to harden.

NOVEMBER

WEEKEND BRUNCH
FOR HOUSEGUESTS
Serves 4

Silver Gin Fizzes
Broiled Grapefruit *
Monte Cristo Sandwich
Cranberry Sauce or Maple Syrup *
Tomato Slices *
Coffee

You are thinking about how many meals your guests are going to need on Sunday before they depart for home. A long, leisurely brunch for the four of you is the best solution for Sunday's food. While your guests are sleeping late and having showers, you can get down to your kitchen alone and fix a pot of coffee, set the dining room table, pick up the Sunday newspaper and start preparations for brunch! This menu is designed so you can assemble it before your guests gather in the kitchen. The cooking takes just a little time, so you can start heating the grapefruit when everyone has appeared in the kitchen and is supplied with a fabulous Silver Gin Fizz.

Table Setting

This is an informal brunch and it would be fun to plan far enough ahead to make a special centerpiece which you can use later in your kitchen. Lacquered bread is easy to make and looks great for years. Bake a batch of different shaped rolls; when cool lacquer them with a paint brush to cover. Pile them in a wicker basket with a bright placement under your basket. A few tartan bows tucked among them will set a festive mood for your brunch. Matching placemats and contrasting napkins will look especially pretty with white ironstone dishes and plain silver. Try utilizing wooden rings used to hang drapes as napkin holders. Your guests will really feel like they have been entertained and will know you have made this a special meal.

*Do ahead

Silver Gin Fizzes

Nothing but the best for your guests. This is for 1 drink.

2 jiggers vodka or gin
1 egg white
1 teaspoon confection-
  ers' sugar
1 tablespoon light
  cream
½ teaspoon orange-
  flower water
juice of ½ lemon
¼ teaspoon vanilla
cracked ice
club soda

Put everything into a blender except club soda; blend until frothy. Use a stemmed wineglass, which has been chilled in the freezer. Top with a little club soda.

Broiled Grapefruit

Very easy and makes grapefruit a little different. Serves 4.

2 grapefruits, cut in
  halves
brown sugar
melted butter

Section and remove any seeds from 4 grapefruit halves. Sprinkle each half with a little brown sugar; drizzle with melted butter. Broil 10 minutes or until golden and heated through.

Monte Cristo Sandwich

This is easy to prepare. The taste is terrific and is very filling. This makes 1 serving.

1 tablespoon butter
3 slices white bread
1 slice cooked ham
2 slices cooked turkey
  or chicken
2 slices Swiss cheese
1 egg
¼ cup milk
2 tablespoons butter

Butter one slice of bread on one side. Place ham slice and sliced chicken or turkey on buttered bread. Spread butter on both sides of second slice of bread; place over meat. Top with cheese slices. Butter third slice of bread on one side. Place on cheese, buttered-side-down. Remove crusts with sharp knife. Cut sandwich in half diagonally; secure with wooden toothpicks. Combine egg and milk in small bowl; blend with rotary beater. Dip sandwich halves into mixture, coating thoroughly. Melt 2 tablespoons butter in skillet. Sauté sandwich on both sides until golden. Remove picks. Serve immediately.

Cranberry Sauce or Maple Syrup

You will enjoy your Monte Cristo with either cranberry sauce or maple syrup or even a cheese sauce. We usually use cranberry sauce.

Tomato Slices

Plain tomato slices will be an excellent accompaniment to the Monte Cristo.

HOME FROM COLLEGE
THANKSGIVING BRUNCH
Serves 12

Cider Punch *
Easy Cheese and Sausage Balls **
Baked Eggs in Tomato Shells *
Baked Ham *
Easy Potatoes *
Miniature Biscuits Supreme *
Marshmallow Treats *
Coffee

When your children come home from college for Thanksgiving they are anxious to see their hometown chums. Inviting everyone for brunch is a super way of getting the group together and assures you of some time with your children. Young appetites appreciate hearty food and this menu is sure to please; as well as tasting good, it is also pleasing to the eye. Since you will be the cook and your son or daughter the host, divide the responsibilities, putting "the host" in charge of refreshments while you prepare the main course in the kitchen. Cooking should be a treat, as your special favorites will pop into the kitchen to chat with you.

Table Setting

Make this table setting easy on yourself. Use your Thanksgiving cornucopia filled with gourds, seasonal fruits and nuts as a centerpiece. Color some paper pennants on small sticks and label with the names of the colleges and universities where the guests attend. Stick these in clay and place near or on the cornucopia and hide the clay with a few leaves. This extra personal touch will be a delight to your guests. Use whatever dishes and flatware seem appropriate for the group. Use TV snack tables, end tables and laps!

*Do ahead
**Freeze

Cider Punch

This can be done ahead of time. If you wish to add applejack, do so when you reheat the punch. Vodka is also good in this. Makes about 14 servings.

6 cups apricot nectar
6 cups apple cider
6 tablespoons sugar
6 tablespoons lemon juice
10 whole cloves

Combine all ingredients in a large saucepan. Bring to a boil, stirring until sugar is dissolved. Flavor is improved if mixture is refrigerated for 1 to 2 days. Reheat to serve.

Easy Cheese and Sausage Balls

This is a great thing to have on hand in your freezer. Very easy and this makes about 200 balls. Freeze before baking.

3½ cups Bisquick
1 pound Cheddar cheese, melted
1 pound bulk sausage (spicy or regular)

Combine above ingredients. Roll into balls the size of a large marble. Place on cookie sheet and bake at 400° for 10-15 minutes.

Baked Eggs In Tomato Shells

This dish tastes as good as it looks. Prepare the tomato shells in advance.

12 medium-ripe firm tomatoes
1½ teaspoons dried basil, crushed
12 eggs
3 ounces processed Swiss cheese, shredded (¾ cup)
¾ cup fine dry bread crumbs
6 tablespoons butter

Cut thin slice from top of each tomato; scoop out pulp. Turn tomatoes upside down to drain for about 10 minutes. Sprinkle tomato shells with a little salt and pepper and the basil; arrange in baking dish, cut-side-up. Break an egg into each shell; sprinkle with a little salt. Bake at 350° for 35 minutes or until egg whites have set. Combine cheese, bread crumbs, and melted butter; sprinkle atop eggs. Return to oven; continue baking until cheese melts and crumbs are browned, about 2 minutes.

Baked Ham

A ham is always a welcome addition to a holiday menu. This is easy and really tastes good. Do ahead. Serves 12 generously.

1 ham (labeled fully
  cooked)
½ cup wine vinegar
2⅔ cups brown sugar
⅔ cup corn flake
  crumbs
Port wine or fruit juice

Soak ham in cold water overnight; drain. Place ham in roasting pan on sheet of foil large enough to wrap completely. Mix 1 quart water, vinegar and 2 cups brown sugar; pour over ham. Fold foil over top. Cover with roasting pan lid. Bake at 300° for 15 minutes per pound. Cool without removing foil. Peel rind and trim fat. Combine crumbs with remaining brown sugar and enough wine to make of spreading consistency. Spread on ham. Bake at 400° for 40 minutes — until sugar is bubbly. Cool before carving.

Easy Potatoes

This was recommended by a friend. It is a handy recipe for company. Serves 12.

12 medium potatoes
  (not Idaho)
1½ pints heavy cream
salt
pepper

Boil potatoes. Peel and grate, while warm, into a 3-quart soufflé or a 3-quart flat baking dish. Salt and pepper. Pour over heavy cream. Refrigerate overnight. Bake 1 hour at 350° uncovered.

Miniature Biscuits Supreme

Especially great with ham. Yield 18-20 tiny biscuits.

2 cups flour, sifted
1½ tablespoons baking
  powder
¼ teaspoon salt
2 tablespoons sugar
½ cup shortening,
  chilled
⅔ cup evaporated milk

Preheat oven to 425°. Sift dry ingredients together. Cut in shortening until mixture resembles coarse crumbs. Add milk all at once and stir until dough follows fork around bowl. Place dough on lightly floured surface, gently patting out dough to ¾-inch thick. Use either small biscuit cutter or a knife which works quite well in getting the desired size and a unique shape. They can be cut into miniature diamonds or any shape desired. Bake at 425° for 10-12 minutes on an ungreased cookie sheet.

Marshmallow Treats

These are easy to make and can be done ahead of time. They will be gobbled up quickly. Yield: 24 squares, 2 × 2 inches.

¼ cup butter
1 package (10 ounces, about 40) regular marshmallows or 4 cups miniature
5 cups Rice Krispies

Melt butter in large saucepan over low heat. Add marshmallows and stir until completely melted. Cook 2 minutes longer, stirring constantly. Remove from heat. Add Rice Krispies. Stir until well coated. Using buttered spatula or waxed paper, press mixture evenly into buttered 13×9×2-inch pan. Cut into squares when cool.

A LARGE PARTY BRUNCH
Serves 40

Sparkling Burgundy Punch *
Spanakotiropetes **
(Spinach-Cheese Puffs)
Fabulous Ham and Cheese Soufflé *
Pears with Raspberry Puree *
Tossed Salad *
Cranberry Coffee Cake **
Coffee and Tea

You have been working on a guest list for a party, and your list grows longer every minute. You are wondering how, when and who? Make it easy on yourself and have fun planning and executing a beautiful brunch to include everyone on your list. You will offer lots of fabulous looking and tasting foods and everything will be done ahead so you can spend time at the party enjoying yourself. Just make sure you get a reliable person or two to help in the kitchen. This way you can just check with them to make sure your plans are being carried out.

Table Setting

For forty people you will probably have to borrow from your family or good friends. Bear in mind the problem of transporting and the damage that might occur. A much easier way is to call your local rental dealer. All you will need are plates, forks and glasses. It will be nice to have white linen napkins wrapped around the fork and tied with a pretty bow and a small hearty flower. Your guests are going to be eating while standing, sitting on chair arms or on the floor, so you will not want to need a knife — the less to carry the better. Make your buffet table look spectacular. A large soup tureen filled with large mums and all your elegant serving dishes will be used. You want your meal to look as good as it tastes, so spend some time and thought on presenting your food.

*Do ahead
**Freeze

Sparkling Burgundy Punch

This is easy and good for a large crowd. This makes about 24 servings. Make this 5 times for 3 drinks per person for 40 people.

1 quart freshly brewed
tea
¼ cup rum
¼ cup cognac
2 lemons, juice of
1 quart sparkling
water, chilled
1 bottle sparkling Bur-
gundy
1 cup sugar syrup
made by briefly boil-
ing 2 cups sugar
with 1 cup water

When the tea has cooled to room temperature, add the rum, cognac and lemon juice. Chill. When ready to serve, pour the mixture into a punch bowl. Add sufficient ice to chill and stir in the sparkling water and sparkling Burgundy. Sweeten to taste with sugar syrup and serve immediately. Float some thin slices of lemon on top for garnish.

Spanakotiropetes (Spinach-Cheese Puffs)

Your guests will have a fabulous treat when they taste one of these spinach-cheese puffs. I just keep a bag of these in my freezer and pop them out for company. They are not the easiest things in the world to make unless you know what you are doing. They take time but are absolutely delicious. This makes about 65 triangles.

2 eggs
1 medium onion, quar-
tered
½ pound Greek feta
cheese, crumbled
1 package (8 ounces)
cream cheese
1 package (10 ounces)
frozen chopped
spinach, thawed
2 tablespoons chopped
parsley
1 tablespoon chopped
fresh dill, or 1 tea-
spoon dill weed
1 package (1 pound)
phyllo or strudel
leaves
1 pound butter, melted

Combine eggs, onion and feta cheese in container of electric blender. Turn to medium speed until smooth; add cream cheese until smooth then pour into a medium size mixing bowl. Squeeze spinach with hands or cheesecloth to remove as much liquid as possible. Add to cheese mixture with parsley and dill; stir until combined thoroughly. Refrigerate a few hours or overnight. Cut end off plastic sleeve which holds the phyllo pastry. Carefully remove a few inches of the pastry from the sleeve and with a sharp knife cut through entire pastry about 1½ inches from end. Replace bulk of pastry in sleeve and close end securely so it will not dry out. Separate and line up about 6 strips and brush generously with melted butter. Cover each strip with another strip of phyllo and brush again with butter. Place about a teaspoon filling on one end of strip.

Fold one corner to opposite side, forming a triangle. Continue folding (like a flag) keeping triangle shape, to other end. Arrange the filled pastries on a flat pan which will fit in your freezer. Repeat with remaining pastry and filling until all is used. Use waxed paper to divide layers. When thoroughly frozen, remove to baggies and put back in freezer. Bake at 375° for 15 minutes or until golden brown. Allow an extra minute or two for baking if frozen. Wait a few minutes before serving — the insides are very, very hot!

Fabulous Ham and Cheese Soufflé

This is so different and so good and so easy. Everyone will want this recipe. Makes 10 servings (quadruple for 40).

16 slices white sandwich-style bread (cut off crusts and cube)
1 pound cubed ham (more or less is fine)
1 pound sharp Cheddar cheese, grated
1½ cups Swiss cheese, cut into small pieces
6 eggs
3 cups milk
½ teaspoon onion salt
½ teaspoon dry mustard
3 cups crushed cornflakes
½ cup butter, melted

Grease 9×13-inch glass baking dish. Spread half the bread cubes evenly in dish. Add the ham and both cheeses, then cover with remaining bread cubes. Mix eggs, milk, onion salt and mustard. Pour evenly over bread cubes and refrigerate overnight. Combine cornflakes and butter for a topping. Bake at 375° for 40 minutes.

Pears With Raspberry Puree

This attractive dish is served cold. Serve on a bed of watercress. Makes 10 servings (quadruple for 40).

10 pear halves
1 package frozen raspberries, defrosted
1 tablespoon sugar
1 teaspoon cornstarch
kirsch (optional)
blanched, slivered almonds

Combine the raspberries with one tablespoon sugar. Mix the cornstarch with two tablespoons cold water and combine with the raspberries. Simmer three minutes and mash through a sieve. Chill and add kirsch to taste. Spoon over the pears and sprinkle with almonds.

Tossed Salad

Do a great big plain salad with different types of lettuce and some spinach. Use your favorite dressing. You will need 6-8 heads of lettuce.

Cranberry Coffee Cake

You will love this great coffee cake. Freezes well. Makes one large cake (make 3 cakes to serve 40).

¼ pound butter
1 cup sugar
2 eggs
1 teaspoon soda
2 cups flour
½ teaspoon salt
½ pint sour cream
1 teaspoon vanilla
1 can (7-8 ounces) whole cranberry sauce
½ cup chopped walnuts

Sauce:

¾ cup powdered sugar
1 tablespoon water
½ teaspoon almond extract

Cream butter and sugar. Add unbeaten eggs, one at a time. Mix dry ingredients. Add alternately with sour cream. Add vanilla and nuts. Pour into a greased 8- or 9-inch tube pan, first a layer of batter, then a layer of cranberry sauce. Repeat ending up with a layer of batter. Bake at 350° for 55 minutes. Cool 5-10 minutes and loosen with knife. Cool on rack. Mix sauce ingredients and drizzle over cake.

DECEMBER

A TREE-TRIMMING BRUNCH
FOR GOOD FRIENDS
Serves 6

Eggnog *
Easy Liver Pâté Mold *
The Great Puffy Pancake
Baked Canadian Bacon *
Watercress-Orange Salad *
Apple Mallow Crisp *
Coffee

One of the nicest traditions you can share with friends is trimming your Christmas tree. It is a good idea to have the lights on the tree and the ornaments and hooks ready before your guests arrive. As special Christmas decorations are opened, you will find yourself reminiscing about Christmases past. There is nothing lovelier than a bowl of traditional eggnog flanked by an elegant Christmas pâté to bolster the Christmas spirit as your friends help trim your tree. The Canadian bacon can be cooked in the morning, taken from the oven and covered with aluminum foil and a terrycloth towel to keep it warm. The preparation for The Great Puffy Pancake is simple. Wait until your guests see what a treat they have in store for them. This is a good opportunity to wear your favorite decorative Christmas apron.

Table Setting

At Christmas time it is nice to give a handmade gift. Nothing could be more appropriate for a tree-trimming party than a Christmas ornament. Making them is fun, and receiving them makes your guests feel very special. Also, you can incorporate them into your table setting.

Start your table setting with a bright red cloth and fresh greens laid on the center of your table. The Christmas balls which you have made can be placed in a wooden sleigh with some small fir pieces to complement them. A few fat Christmas candles can be placed around the sleigh. White napkins tied with a Christmas ribbon and a small bell or shiny ornament can be placed at each setting. If you are lucky enough to have Christmas dishes, by all means use them.

*Do ahead
**Freeze

Eggnog

Very filling and very smooth! Easy to prepare. This makes six servings.

6 eggs
½ cup sugar
2 cups milk
1 cup light rum
1 teaspoon nutmeg
dash salt

In covered blender container, blend all ingredients at low speed until well mixed.

Easy Liver Pâté Mold

This is a very easy mold and very delicious. This can serve 14-16 for an appetizer with cocktails and additional hors d'oeuvres. Since this is the only appetizer in this menu and since you will be tree-trimming here, make the whole thing for 6.

3 cans (4¾ ounces each) liver pâté (Sells is good)
1 large can (4½ ounces) deviled ham
1 large package (8 ounces) cream cheese, softened
sherry to taste
onions, chopped for garnish
hard pumpernickel or whole grain bread
parsley

Combine all ingredients well. Line a small bowl with a large piece of plastic wrap. Spoon in mixture and pull plastic wrap over top to cover. Refrigerate. Unmold on serving dish. Use hands to pat onions over entire mold. Garnish with parsley. Cut bread into triangles and arrange attractively around pâté mold.

The Great Puffy Pancake

This was suggested to me by a very nice tennis friend. I now use it all the time for guests and my family. Wait until you see what happens when the 20 minutes in the oven is up! This is a little different and your guests will rave. Easy to make. Serves 3 (double this for 6 and use two skillets).

½ cup flour
½ cup milk
2 eggs, slightly beaten
pinch nutmeg

4 tablespoons butter
2 tablespoons confectioners' sugar
juice of ½ lemon

Preheat oven to 425°. Mix flour, eggs, milk and nutmeg together, leaving batter a bit lumpy. Melt butter in large frying pan and add the batter. Bake 15-20 minutes until golden brown. Sprinkle with confectioners' sugar and return briefly to oven. Sprinkle with lemon juice. Cut into wedges.

Baked Canadian Bacon

Delicious. Serves 6.

3 pounds whole Canadian bacon
½ cup brown sugar
1 tablespoon prepared mustard
dash allspice
1 cup pineapple or orange juice

Remove casing from bacon. Mix sugar, mustard and allspice; spread over top of bacon. Bake on a rack in oven pan at 325° for 35 minutes to the pound. Baste often with juice.

Watercress-Orange Salad

This is a lovely combination. Serves 6-8.

2 bunches watercress
3 heads Belgian endive
2 oranges
2 shallots, finely chopped
⅓ cup olive oil
2 tablespoons lemon juice
salt and pepper to taste

Wash, trim and cut watercress into small pieces. Place in a large bowl. Cut endive in ¼-inch pieces. Peel and section oranges. Add endive and orange sections to watercress. Combine remaining ingredients; pour over salad. Toss gently.

Apple Mallow Crisp

This looks lovely topped with golden miniature marshmallows. Easily prepared. Serves 6.

4 cups sliced and
   peeled apples
¼ cup raisins
¼ cup water
¾ cup flour
½ cup sugar
1 teaspoon cinnamon
¼ teaspoon salt
1 stick (8 tablespoons)
   butter
1½ cups miniature
   marshmallows

Place apples, raisins and water in 10x6-inch baking dish. Combine flour, sugar, cinnamon and salt. Cut in butter until mixture resembles coarse crumbs; sprinkle over apples. Bake at 350° for 35-40 minutes or until apples are tender. Sprinkle evenly with marshmallows. Broil until lightly browned.

CAROLING PARTY BRUNCH
Serves 12

Wassail Bowl *

Rumaki **
(Chicken Livers and Chestnuts
Wrapped in Bacon)

Cheese Delights **

Turkey-Spinach Crepes **

Cucumber-Lime Salad Mold *

Carrot Cake **

Assorted Christmas Cookies
(Kourambiedes) **
(Tasty Macaroons) **
(Luscious Lemon Squares) **

Coffee

Between Christmas shopping and partying, take some time for the real spirit of Christmas. Caroling for shut-ins (possibly ill or older members of your church) will give more meaning to the Christmas holidays. Have the group meet after the mid-morning church service. Ask the minister for names and have him call ahead to advise people that you are coming and to tell them what approximate time your group will arrive. The carolers will welcome a warm Wassail Bowl when they return to your house for brunch. If you have a piano player in your group, he or she will probably be only too happy to lead the carolers in song while everyone enjoys the hot Wassail Bowl, Rumaki and Cheese Delights. Your entire menu has been prepared ahead, so you will just need time to get things in the oven and set things out on your buffet table.

Table Setting

A wide red-felt runner cut the length of your table and placed over a white linen tablecloth will show off your centerpiece. Carolers made of ceramic, wood or paper clustered with lots of different-sized candles will be appropriate for the occasion. If you can find a music scroll, fit it into the arrangement. A really easy holiday napkin holder can be made at home and saved from year to year. Cut 1-inch wide strips of red felt and sew on snaps or Velcro to make a ring. You can purchase a package of tiny felt Christmas trimmings or make up your own small arrangement to sew onto the top of the napkin ring. Your special cut salad trees from the Cucumber-Lime Salad Mold will further carry out your Christmas theme.

 *Do ahead
**Freeze

Wassail Bowl

This traditional holiday drink can be made with liquor or without. Makes 36 servings.

3 large cooking apples, cored
1 gallon apple cider
6 whole cloves
6 whole allspice
2 teaspoons nutmeg
1 can (6 ounces) frozen lemonade concentrate
1 can (16 ounces) frozen orange juice concentrate
1 cup packed brown sugar
OR:
1 quart cider (instead of 1 gallon)
2 bottles (1 quart each) ale
1 bottle dry sherry

Preheat oven to 350°. Cut apples in half crosswise and place, cut-sides-down, in 9×13-inch baking dish. Bake 25 minutes. Simmer 2 cups apple cider, cloves, allspice and nutmeg 10 minutes. Add remaining apple cider (or ale and sherry), lemonade and orange juice concentrates and brown sugar. Heat until hot but not boiling, stirring occasionally. Pour hot mixture into heated large punch bowl. Float apples, skin-sides-up. You may wish to add a cinnamon stick to each serving.

Rumaki
(Chicken livers and chestnuts wrapped in bacon)

These are ideal for a brunch. They can be all done but the cooking and then frozen. Makes 24.

12 chicken livers, halved at the natural separation
24 slices water chestnuts
12 slices bacon, cut in half crosswise
1½ cups soy sauce
1 clove garlic, minced
1 cup light brown sugar

Make a small incision in center of each piece of chicken liver and insert a slice of water chestnut. Wrap each with a half strip of bacon and secure with a toothpick. Mix rest of ingredients and marinate bacon roll-ups in the refrigerator for several hours. Remove from marinade and roll lightly in brown sugar. Broil about 10 minutes, turning once.

Cheese Delights

This is really easy and really good. Makes 48. Freezes well.

6 plain or onion
  English muffins,
  halved and buttered
4 ounces grated sharp
  Cheddar cheese
4 ounces grated
  mozzarella cheese
¾ cup mayonnaise

Make a paste of the cheeses and mayonnaise and spread on split and buttered English muffins. Cut in quarters and broil until bubbly and light golden brown.

Turkey-Spinach Crepes

These can also be made with chicken. However, I think the flavor is better with turkey. Just follow the directions to freeze below. These crepes are rolled quite thin, so plan to serve 3 per person. This recipe makes 36 crepes.

Crepes:
1 cup cold water
1 cup cold milk
4 eggs
½ teaspoon salt
2 cups sifted flour
4 tablespoons butter,
  melted

Filling:
6 tablespoons butter
3 onions, chopped
1 pound mushrooms,
  sliced thin
1 package (10 ounces)
  frozen chopped
  spinach, cooked and
  drained well
3 cups chopped cooked
  turkey
6 tablespoons sour
  cream
3 tablespoons sherry
½ teaspoon salt
dash cayenne

Crepes: Place all ingredients in blender at high speed for 1 minute. Refrigerate at least 2 hours. Place pan (makes 5½-inch crepes) over heat, brush with a little oil and when almost smoking add batter, tilting pan to get batter all over bottom. Shake pan to loosen crepe and when lightly browned, turn by flipping with a spatula. Cook briefly on this side and turn out of pan. Stack crepes with waxed paper, aluminum foil or paper towel between them.

Filling: Heat butter in large skillet, add onion and sauté until onions are transparent. Add mushrooms and cook 4 minutes, stirring occasionally. Stir in turkey and all other ingredients. Remove from heat and cool.

Sauce:

4 tablespoons butter
4 tablespoons flour
2 cups chicken broth
1 cup milk
½ cup grated Parmesan cheese
½ cup grated Swiss cheese
salt to taste
dash cayenne
⅛ teaspoon saffron
½ cup sherry

Sauce: Melt butter in pan; blend in flour. Add broth and milk; blend well and bring to boil to thicken. Add cheeses and seasonings and continue cooking until cheeses have melted and are well blended. Remove from heat and add sherry.

Place ¼ cup of filling at one end of crepe and roll up into tubular shape, making sure some of the filling reaches ends. Place in a greased baking dish. Place 1 tablespoon of the sauce over each and bake at 350° for 15 minutes. Pour remaining sauce over crepes and bake another 15 minutes.

To freeze: Freeze rolled crepes and sauce separately. Thaw sauce completely before cooking. Thaw crepes at room temperature 1 hour before cooking. Place one tablespoon of sauce over each crepe. Bake partially thawed crepes at 350° for 25 minutes. Pour remaining sauce and bake another 15 minutes.

Cucumber-Lime Salad Mold

This recipe has been my mother's favorite and mine for years. Everyone asks for it. For the holidays, you can double this recipe and put it into an 8- or 9-inch round cake pan and cut the pieces into pie shapes. These will look like trees, and you can add a few pieces of parsley and cut pimento for decorations. Serve on a bed of curly lettuce. This recipe serves 6 (double for 12).

1 small package (3 ounces) lime gelatin
1 cup hot water
1 cup chopped celery
1 cucumber, chopped & partially peeled
1 small red onion, chopped
1 cup cottage cheese
¾ cup mayonnaise
1 tablespoon lemon juice
salt; pepper

Dissolve gelatin in 1 cup hot water. Add rest of ingredients and stir (I use a whisk) until blended. Pour into small greased mold. Chill.

Carrot Cake

This is delicious any time of the year. Freezes well and is easy to make. Makes approximately 16 servings.

2 cups raw grated car-
  rots
3 cups flour
2 cups sugar
2 teaspoons baking
  powder
1 teaspoon soda
1 teaspoon salt
1 teaspoon nutmeg
2 teaspoons cinnamon
1 cup chopped nuts
4 eggs
1½ cups oil
1 teaspoon vanilla

Icing:

⅓ cup lemon juice
2 cups confectioners'
  sugar

Mix all dry ingredients (first 9). Add eggs, oil and vanilla. Bake in an angel food cake pan at 325° for 1 hour.

Icing: Combine lemon juice and confectioners' sugar and beat well. While cake is still hot and still in pan, poke all over with a metal ice pick or skewer and pour on icing. Age at least 24 hours before serving.

Kourambiedes (Christmas butter cookies)

These will be eaten so quickly you will not believe it! Makes 4 dozen.

2 cups sweet butter, at
  room temperature
confectioners' sugar
1 egg yolk
1½ tablespoons cognac
  or brandy
4½ cups cake flour,
  sifted twice
whole cloves

Cream the butter in an electric mixer until thick and lemon-colored. Sift ¾ cup confectioners' sugar and add it gradually to the butter. Add egg yolk, creaming well. Add cognac. Gradually work in the flour to make a soft dough that will roll easily in the palm of the hand without sticking. If sticky, refrigerate the dough for 1 hour. Preheat oven to 350°. Pat and shape the dough into balls 1½ inches in diameter. Stud each cake with a whole clove. Place on ungreased baking sheet and bake until sandy colored (not brown), about 15 minutes. Cool and sift over generously with confectioners' sugar.

Tasty Macaroons

These are very light, chewy and wonderful! Easy to prepare. Makes 15-20 cookies.

1 egg white
1 cup light brown
   sugar (packed)
¼ teaspoon salt
½ teaspoon vanilla
½ cup chopped pecans

Preheat oven to 325°. Butter and flour cookie sheet. Beat egg white until foamy. Gradually beat in brown sugar. Continue beating until mixture is stiff and glossy. Fold in nuts. Drop from a teaspoon on cookie sheet. Bake 12 minutes.

Luscious Lemon Squares

A real treat. I usually double this recipe and use a 16x12-inch pan which makes the squares extra thin. These freeze very well and taste better if served cold. Makes approximately 3-dozen small squares.

½ cup butter
1 cup flour, sifted
¼ cup confectioners'
   sugar

Filling:

2 tablespoons lemon
   juice
1 lemon rind, grated
2 eggs, well beaten
1 cup sugar
2 tablespoons flour
½ teaspoon baking
   powder

Frosting:

¾ cup confectioners'
   sugar
1 teaspoon vanilla
1 tablespoon butter
1 tablespoon milk
1 cup shredded
   coconut

Preheat oven to 350°. Mix ½ cup butter with 1 cup flour and add ¼ cup confectioners' sugar. Press mixture into bottom of 9-inch square pan. Bake for 12 minutes. Cool for 15 minutes.

Filling: Blend ingredients together well. Place on baked layer. Bake for 25 minutes. Cool for 30 minutes.

Frosting: Blend all ingredients thoroughly. Spread over filling. Cut into small squares to serve.

NEIGHBORHOOD PARTY BRUNCH
Serves 24

Company Eggnog *

Sliced Fruitcake with
Watermelon Pickle *

Company Quiche Lorraine *

Cranberry-Raspberry Salad Mold *

Caesar Salad *

Cheese Cupcakes **

Coffee and Tea

Everyone is feeling in a festive mood between Christmas and New Year. You have spent much time decorating your house for the holidays; Christmas is over and you are anxious to have some people in to see all your trimmings. The brunch is the answer for your young, old, single or married neighbors. Your house looks its best at Christmas and since it is already decorated, all you have to think about is the food and rearranging all the presents attractively under the tree. The menu can be done ahead, so you can cook at your own pace. The food is easy to prepare for this size group, and requires only a plate, fork and napkin which is important when guests will be eating from plastic plates on their laps.

Table Setting

Use your traditional Christmas dinner centerpiece to decorate your buffet table. If you have a Christmas tablecloth, this is a good opportunity to use it. If necessary, borrow china plates and forks from one of your neighbors. Plastic Christmas glasses can be used for the Eggnog and decorated paper hot cups will do the trick for coffee. Of course you will use paper Christmas cocktail napkins and heavy paper dinner napkins which are available in plain colors or with a pretty Christmas motif. Make sure your tree lights are on and all your Christmas candles are lit for the brunch as this creates a lovely holiday mood.

*Do ahead
**Freeze

Company Eggnog

A merry old way to celebrate the holidays. Makes 50 punch-cup servings.

15 egg yolks
2½ cups sugar
½ teaspoon salt
1 quart heavy cream
2 quarts milk
1 quart bourbon
1 pint rye whiskey
½ pint sherry
¾ pint dark Jamaica
  rum
15 egg whites
nutmeg

Separate eggs and place whites in refrigerator. Blend together sugar, salt and egg yolks; beat until frothy. Let stand. Whip cream and let stand. Add milk to egg mixture; blend well. Combine bourbon, rye, sherry, rum and whipped cream; blend thoroughly and let stand. Whip egg whites until stiff and fold into mixture. Stir vigorously with long-handled wooden spoon. Mixture should develop small "islands." Refrigerate and ripen for about 3 or 4 hours. Serve with grated nutmeg.

Sliced Fruitcake With Watermelon Pickle

It is always nice to have this delicious cake around for the holidays. Makes 2 loaves.

3 cups sifted all-
  purpose flour
1½ teaspoons baking
  powder
½ teaspoon salt
7 ounces candied red
  and green cherries,
  halved
6 ounces candied
  pineapple, shredded
4 ounces candied
  lemon, shredded
2 cups drained
  watermelon pickle,
  shredded
12 ounces white raisins
6½ ounces pecans,
  chopped
4½ ounces almonds,
  blanched, shredded
  and toasted
1 cup butter

½ cup sherry
2 cups sugar
5 eggs

Preheat oven to 300°. Grease two 9×5×3-inch loaf pans, line with waxed paper and grease the paper. Sift together the flour, baking powder and salt. Mix several tablespoons of this mixture into fruits and nuts. Cream the butter until smooth, adding sugar gradually. Add the eggs, one at a time, beating well after each. Stir in the flour mixture alternately with sherry. Mix in fruit-nut mixture. Transfer batter to pans, pressing down. Bake 2 hours. Cool, remove from pans and peel off paper. Wrap the cakes in foil and store them in an airtight container about one month before serving. Sprinkle several times a week with a light shower of sherry.

Company Quiche Lorraine

This is easy to do and can be done a day or two in advance. Just reheat at 350° for 20 minutes or until hot. The freezer pie shells are a little smaller than the usual homemade pie shell. I use the frozen 9-inch pie shells and love them — they are a real help when making four pies! Cut each pie into 6 sections, which is a good size portion for everyone. If you only need 2 or 3, freeze the rest. Serves 24.

4 frozen 9-inch pie shells

1 pound bacon, cooked, drained and crumbled

4 medium onions, sliced thin

1¼ pounds grated Gruyère or Swiss cheese

1 cup grated Parmesan cheese

10 eggs, slightly beaten

2½ cups heavy cream

1¾ cups milk

1 teaspoon salt

½ teaspoon white pepper

1 teaspoon nutmeg

Bake pie shell according to directions on package 8-10 minutes. Cook the sliced onions in a little bacon fat until the onions are translucent. Sprinkle the bacon, onion and cheeses over the inside of the partly baked pie shells. Combine the eggs, cream, milk, salt, pepper and nutmeg and pour over the onion-cheese mixture. Bake the pies 15 minutes at 450°, reduce the oven temperature to 350° and bake 10 minutes longer. Cool. Cover with plastic wrap and refrigerate. Bake at 350° til hot — about 20 minutes.

Cranberry-Raspberry Salad Mold

This is a lovely mold for any special occasion. You may wish to use a disposable angel food cake-type pan. Do this a day or two in advance. Serves 12 (double for 24).

1 large package (6 ounces) raspberry gelatin

1 small package (3 ounces) lemon gelatin

2 cups boiling water

1 package (10 ounces) frozen raspberries

1 jar (14 ounces) cranberry orange relish

1 can (1 pound 4 ounces) crushed pineapple

Dissolve gelatin in boiling water. Add frozen raspberries and stir until melted. Add rest of ingredients and mix well. Pour into pan or mold. Chill until firm.

Caesar Salad

This is a real favorite and can be done ahead except for the tossing. Serves 8 people. When tripling recipe make sure you use a very large glass or wooden bowl.

2 heads romaine lettuce

¼ teaspoon dry mustard

¼ teaspoon pepper

1 teaspoon salt

½ cup grated Parmesan cheese

1 garlic clove, halved

6 tablespoons olive oil

2 lemons, juice of

2 eggs, raw

2 cups croutons

6 anchovy fillets, cut in pieces

If you are planning to do this ahead of time, measure out all the ingredients and put into small containers and baggies. Soak your garlic in olive oil and then discard clove before adding to salad. Use a large plastic bag for your cleaned and torn romaine lettuce and keep refrigerated. Before serving, put everything into a large bowl (except the croutons and anchovies) and toss lightly but thoroughly. Then add your croutons and anchovies on top and toss lightly.

Cheese Cupcakes

These are like a cheesecake, but they are easier to serve because they are done as cupcakes. You will not need a dessert plate. They will look especially nice for the holidays if you serve them topped with red and green glazed cherries and arranged on a platter. Makes 24. Freeze what you do not use.

3 large packages (8 ounces each) cream cheese

1 cup sugar

5 eggs

1 teaspoon vanilla

Topping:

½ pint sour cream

2 tablespoons sugar

½ teaspoon vanilla

24 red or green (or both) glazed cherries

Combine cream cheese, 1 cup sugar, 5 eggs and vanilla and blend until smooth. Line muffin tins with cupcake papers, fill each ⅔ full. Bake at 300° for 45 minutes. Remove from oven and when cakes sink (about 5 minutes) top each with 1 teaspoon of topping (combined sour cream, sugar and vanilla). Put back in oven for 5-10 minutes.

AN ALL-OCCASION BRUNCH
FOR ANY SEASON

Orange Refreshers

Swedish Meatballs**

Crabmeat on Cucumber Slices*

Asparagus-Lobster Cocktail Mold*

Chicken Livers Divan*

Ham Mousse Ring Filled with
Creamed Eggs*

Cheese Noodle Omelet

Potato Pancakes*

Applesauce-Raspberry Salad Mold*

Tiny Caramel Swirls**

Apricot Brandy Pound Cake**

Easy Blueberry and Cherry Cream
Cheese Tarts*

This elegant brunch will satisfy all palates, as you have a great variety of tempting dishes. Everyone can choose his favorite foods from this diverse selection. Do not try to have enough of each item for everyone — different people have different tastes. If you do not wish to prepare all of these, choose the ones you think your guests will enjoy most.

Table Setting
This should be served buffet-style, using whatever is seasonably correct for decorations and china.

*Do ahead
**Freeze

Orange Refreshers

This is really nothing more than a watered-down orange juice. Use any size glass you wish for this light and refreshing beverage.

orange juice
crushed ice
water

Almost fill any size glass with crushed ice. Fill half way with orange juice and top with water.

Swedish Meatballs

These bring raves everytime they are served. They can also be made into a much larger meatball and served as a main course with wild rice. Although the meatballs freeze well, do not try to freeze the sauce. They can also be served as appetizers without the sauce. Be sure you make plenty. Makes approximately 75 meatballs.

6 tablespoons butter
½ cup instant minced onion
½ pound round steak, ½ pound veal, ½ pound pork (have butcher grind together)
2 eggs, slightly beaten
2 teaspoons salt
¼ teaspoon pepper
2 teaspoons Worcestershire sauce
2 slices bread, soaked in milk and wrung out

Sauce:

1½ cups sour cream
¼ cup heavy cream
2 teaspoons dill seed
½ teaspoon salt

Melt 2 tablespoons butter in skillet. Add onion and sauté until golden brown; be careful not to burn. Put meat into a large mixing bowl and add eggs, sautéed onions, salt, pepper, Worcestershire sauce and soaked bread. Mix well and shape into one-inch balls. In a heavy skillet, melt 4 tablespoons butter and sauté meatballs on all sides until done. Drain fat from skillet. Add all sauce ingredients to skillet and heat but do not let boil.

Serve meatballs with sauce and toothpicks.

Crabmeat on Cucumber Slices

What a light and refreshing taste! These will disappear before you have a chance to put the tray down. Makes approximately 24.

1 can (7½ ounces) king
   crabmeat, drained
   and flaked
½ cup celery, chopped
   fine
1 tablespoon
   mayonnaise
2 tablespoons ketchup
1 package (3 ounces)
   cream cheese
1 teaspoon
   Worcestershire
   sauce
salt
pepper
paprika
cucumber slices

Combine all ingredients and chill. Spread on chilled ¼-inch-thick cucumber slices.

Asparagus-Lobster Cocktail Mold

Guests are always trying to guess at the ingredients in this marvelous appetizer. I use a fish-shaped porcelain mold and arrange thin hard pumpernickel or whole grain bread around the unmolded fish, which is sitting in a bed of parsley. (I have not had good luck doing this in a metal mold, since it turns rancid.) You can unmold this hours before your guests arrive and just refrigerate until ready to serve. 35 servings.

1½ cups canned
   asparagus (cuts and
   tips)
2 envelopes unflavored
   gelatin
1 can cream of
   asparagus soup
3 packages (8 ounces
   each) cream cheese
1 teaspoon celery seed
½ cup finely chopped
   onion
1 cup mayonnaise

1 can (12 ounces)
   frozen lobster
   chunks, thawed and
   drained
½ teaspoon salt

Puree asparagus in blender with ¼ cup asparagus liquid. Sprinkle gelatin on ½ cup lobster liquid or water. Heat soup and cream cheese together over low heat, stirring until smooth. Add puree, gelatin and rest of ingredients and mix well. Pour into oiled 2-quart mold. Serve with a spreader.

Chicken Livers Divan

A very different and delicious way to serve chicken livers. This can be cooked and assembled the day ahead and heated before serving. Serves 6.

3 packages frozen
  broccoli, partially
  cooked and drained
1½ pounds chicken
  livers, dredged in
  seasoned flour and
  sautéed in butter
½ pound bacon,
  cooked and
  crumbled

Sauce:
1 cup mayonnaise
1 cup sour cream
½ cup grated Parmesan
  cheese

In a casserole, layer broccoli, chicken livers and crumbled bacon. Mix sauce ingredients and pour over casserole. Bake at 350° uncovered. Before serving, sprinkle with paprika and parsley.

Ham Mousse Ring Filled with Creamed Eggs

A delectable dish which really looks lovely on a buffet table. Serves 12.

4 cups cooked ground
  ham
2 cups bread or cracker
  crumbs or crushed
  cornflakes
2 eggs
4 tablespoons chili
  sauce
2 cups grated carrots
2 cups milk

Creamed Eggs (Follow directions for Creamed Eggs with Ham on page 14, leaving out ham).

Combine ham, crumbs, eggs, chili sauce, carrots and milk. Grease a 2-quart ring mold and fill with mixture. Bake at 350° for 50 minutes. Unmold onto a platter and fill cavity with creamed eggs. Decorate mold with fresh parsley.

Cheese Noodle Omelet

A wonderful and slightly different way to do eggs. Serves 8.

8 eggs, more than
  slightly beaten
1 teaspoon salt
dash pepper
2 tablespoons chopped
  green pepper

1 tablespoon pimiento
2 tablespoons butter,
  melted
2 cups cooked noodles
1 cup shredded
  Cheddar cheese

Melt butter in large skillet. Combine all ingredients and mix well. Add mixture to skillet. Cover and cook over medium heat 15-20 minutes. Do not stir. Cut into wedges and remove from skillet.

Potato Pancakes

These go well with so many things and are easy to prepare. Makes about 25.

**3 medium raw
   potatoes, grated
1 tablespoon flour or
   bread crumbs
1 tablespoon cream
   (sweet or sour)
1 egg, slightly beaten
1 teaspoon salt
2 onions, grated**

Mix all ingredients together. Cook by spoonfuls in shallow hot fat. Turn once. Great with applesauce.

Applesauce-Raspberry Salad Mold

A "surprise" gelatin mold. Serves 12.

**2 cups applesauce
1 large package (6
   ounces) raspberry
   gelatin
14 ounces lemon-lime
   carbonated beverage
1 large can crushed
   pineapple
½ cup chopped pecans
   (optional)**

Heat applesauce and add gelatin, stirring until dissolved. Cool to lukewarm. Stir in carbonated beverage. Drain pineapple and add along with pecans to gelatin mixture. Pour into mold and chill.

Tiny Caramel Swirls

An absolutely delicious hot bread which can be completely finished and then frozen. Reheat at 350° until hot — about 20 minutes, covered. My good friend suggested putting the bowl of yeast on a heating pad turned to low — it works very well. Makes approximately 80.

2 yeast cakes
½ cup flour
½ cup lukewarm water
½ cup lukewarm milk
1½ teaspoons sugar
½ cup butter, softened
½ cup sugar
½ teaspoon salt
2 eggs, beaten
1 teaspoon vanilla
4 cups flour, sifted
melted butter
brown sugar
cinnamon
1 cup butter
1 cup brown sugar
2 tablespoons light
    corn syrup
1 cup finely chopped
    pecans

Crumble yeast over ½ cup flour. Add ¼ cup water, ¼ cup milk and 1½ teaspoons sugar. Stir well. Cover and let stand in a warm place for 20 minutes. Beat ½ cup butter and gradually add ½ cup sugar. Continue beating until creamy. Add ½ teaspoon salt, 2 eggs, ¼ cup water, ¼ cup milk and vanilla. Add one-half of the flour to the batter, then add yeast mixture, then remaining flour. Knead well. Cover and let rise 1½-2 hours. Cut into 4 portions and roll into oblongs. (Approximately 16 × 10 inches). Brush on melted butter and sprinkle with brown sugar and a little cinnamon. Roll each oblong separately, rolling the long edges to each other jelly roll-style. Cut each section into about 20 slices. Melt together 1 cup butter, 1 cup brown sugar, 2 tablespoons corn syrup and 1 cup chopped pecans. Divide mixture into 4 cake pans (8 or 9-inch size). You should get about 20 swirls into each pan. Bake at 350° for 15 minutes.

Apricot Brandy Pound Cake

Lots of ingredients, but delicious and easy.

3 cups sugar
1 cup butter
6 eggs
3 cups flour
¼ teaspoon baking
    soda
½ teaspoon salt
1 cup sour cream
1 teaspoon orange
    flavoring

1 teaspoon vanilla
    flavoring
½ teaspoon rum
    flavoring
½ teaspoon lemon
    flavoring
¼ teaspoon almond
    flavoring
½ cup apricot brandy

Grease and flour a large tube pan. Cream butter and sugar. Add eggs one at a time. Sift flour, baking soda and salt. Combine sour cream, flavorings and brandy. Add flavorings and flour mixture alternately to cream mixture. Mix just until blended. Bake 325° for 70—80 minutes.

Easy Blueberry and Cherry Cream Cheese Tarts

Perfect for a crowd and so easy. Makes 24.

3 large packages (8 ounces each) cream cheese
½ cup sugar
2 eggs
1 teaspoon vanilla
1½ cups graham cracker crumbs
¼ cup sugar
¼ cup butter, melted
1 can blueberry pie filling
1 can cherry pie filling

Beat first four ingredients until creamy. Mix crumbs, sugar and butter and portion evenly into paper-lined cup pan (muffin tin). Add cream cheese filling. Top half with blueberry pie filling and the other half with cherry pie filling. Bake at 375° for 10 minutes. Refrigerate.

Index

BREADS

PANCAKES AND FRENCH TOASTS

CAKES

COOKIES AND CONFECTIONS

OTHER DESSERTS

EGGS AND CHEESE

FRUIT

MEATS AND POULTRY

SEAFOOD

MOLDED SALADS

SALADS

SANDWICHES

SAUCES

Hollandaise Sauce 64,90
Sauce Florentine 49
Strawberry Sauce 30

SOUPS

Asparagus-Leek Soup 93
Chilled Watercress Soup 75
Hot or Cold Vichyssoise 91
Oyster Bisque 10
Split Pea Soup 107

VEGETABLES

Cold Artichokes with Hollandaise Sauce 90
Cold Tomatoes with Mushrooms and Artichokes 54
Crudités 18
Easy Potatoes 121
Fresh Asparagus 64
Oven Tomatoes with Cornflakes 49
Raw Broccoli and Dip 107
Tomatoes Stuffed with Mushrooms 15
Tomato Wedges 101

Notes

Notes

Notes

Table of Measures

LIQUID* METRIC CONVERSIONS

1 teaspoon	5 milliliters
1 tablespoon (3 teaspoons)	15 milliliters
1 ounce (2 tablespoons)	30 milliliters
¼ cup	60 milliliters
⅓ cup	75 milliliters
½ cup (4 ounces)	125 milliliters
1 cup (8 ounces)	250 milliliters (¼ liter)
2 cups (1 pint)	500 milliliters (½ liter)
4 cups (1 quart)	1000 milliliters (1 liter)

*metric equivalents slightly rounded

DRY METRIC CONVERSION

½ teaspoon	2½ grams
1 teaspoon	5 grams
1 tablespoon	14 grams
1 ounce	28 grams
4 ounces (¼ pound)	113 grams
8 ounces (½ pound)	226 grams
16 ounces (1 pound)	500 grams